T0365152

Advice for the Next Generation

For

Carole, Brianna, Courtney and Yvette

Advice for the Next Generation

This is a true account of my life.

Some names have been changed to protect identities.

Order this book online at www.trafford.com
or email orders@trafford.com

Most Trafford titles are also available at major online book retailers.

Print information available on the last page.

ISBN: 978-1-4120-4232-1 (sc)

Trafford rev. 12/05/2024

www.trafford.com

North America & international
toll-free: 844-688-6899 (USA & Canada)
fax: 812 355 4082

Contents

Preface

When I first started writing this book, I wanted to share my thoughts about the mistakes I had made in life, and what I had learned as a result of them. I hoped that by telling how I had gotten into certain situations, I could help others recognize when things were going bad. If they knew what to look for, maybe they would make better decisions than I did. Maybe they wouldn't experience the same pains I had been through. Along the way, I came to the understanding that everyone is going to make mistakes, because that is what makes us human. It is in our mistakes that we can learn the most, although some people never seem to learn and they continually repeat the same mistakes over and over again. Other people learn from both their mistakes and those made by others, and they use that knowledge to avoid putting themselves in more bad situations. This book is for those people. By reading about the bad decisions I made in my life, and the consequences I experienced because of them, perhaps they can have fewer problems to deal with in their lives. Life is a complicated enough process without having extreme problems to face.

I am thirty-one years old now, and I have been divorced twice, been bankrupted, been cheated out of money, and have lost a few good friends along the way. My coworker and good friend, Chuck, once described my life as a soap opera, and in many ways he is right. Life can be that way, but it is often a result of how we choose to live. The decisions I made in my earlier years created the life I had and the decisions I make today are more informed, and make for a better life today. I can draw on my experiences and from the people around me, so I don't make as many bad decisions as I did in the past. That is why I decided to write this book. I wanted to tell young people that life is about the choices they make. Sometimes things just happen to us, things that are beyond our control, but most of life is not that way. We can control our destiny to a point. Our choices can help us or hurt us, and it is up to us to take responsibility for our lives. We can make the right choices, and we can live with fewer headaches and heartaches. We can't eliminate them, because we are only human, but we can learn to make fewer mistakes. That is the reason I decided to write about the trials and tribulations of my life, to open the closet door and pull the skeletons out for everyone to see. I figured that if I reached a few people, and they didn't repeat some of the mistakes I made, they would live better lives. If that happened, then exposing my errors to the world was worth it.

Don't sign away your rights

I was conned when I was twenty-one. I had taken out an unsecured personal loan from a bank, and had used the money to purchase an older Jeep CJ-5. The Jeep was fun transportation, when it worked, but it was not practical. In the summer it was hot to drive and in the winter it was freezing. It broke down on me pretty regularly, and for someone starting a family as I was at the time, the Jeep was just not the right vehicle. When I bought a more reliable mode of transportation, a slightly used Chevy Cavalier, I didn't like the small amount of money that was offered for the Jeep as a trade-in. I decided to sell the Jeep on my own rather than take the small amount the car lot offered.

I knew a guy who I'll call Dan. He had moved to town with my half-sister and was introduced to the family by her. When she decided to move back to Ohio, he stayed here. I had only known him for a couple of months, but he seemed like an honest enough guy. He'd gotten a job at a car wash on one of the busiest streets in town, and he had rented a place in a trailer park that had a community pool. I was hanging around him periodically so I had free access to the pool, but also because he knew very few people out here and had no one to talk to outside of work. About a week after I'd bought the Cavalier I was at Dan's place in the afternoon and we got to talking about how I was going to sell the Jeep. If I drove the Jeep to my work it would be parked on a seldom traveled side-street where very few people would see it and it would probably take a while to sell. Dan suggested that I let him drive the Jeep to his work everyday and he would park it out front with a "For Sale" sign on it. Dan said he could get it cleaned up and waxed for free, would keep it washed regularly and he could park it where it would be highly visible. This seemed like a pretty good arrangement as far as I was concerned, so Dan started driving the Jeep to work everyday.

About a week later, Dan called me in the evening and said that he'd had two people who were interested in buying the Jeep, but one wanted to get it that day and Dan could not sell it since I had not notarized the title. The other person interested in the Jeep was someone Dan worked with. Dan convinced me to sign over the title and get it notarized, so that if he had a buyer he could sell it right then and could just bring me the money. This is where I made my mistake. I signed over the title to the Jeep.

A couple days later, Dan called me to say that he had sold the Jeep to the guy he worked with, and that the guy had given him $600 for a down payment and would pay Dan the rest at the end of the week. I collected the $600 from Dan, but that was the only money I ever saw. Dan left town the following day, and as it turned out, the guy he'd sold the Jeep to did not work with him. I never did know who bought the Jeep, but they had a legally signed and notarized title.

Dan never did turn up anywhere that I ever heard of. I suppose he went back to Ohio, but he was nowhere that I could reach him to get what was owed to me. I still owed the bank about $1800 and I had to pay that off. It took a while, but I did pay them because I was responsible for it. I learned from this experience that a person should never sign away their ownership rights to something until after they have been compensated. Whether you have just met the person you're dealing with or you have known them for years, you have to protect yourself and should never make the mistake of signing away ownership without compensation. I made this mistake, and it cost me.

Get all the details

My first wife, Mary, and I were struggling with the bills we had with only my income supporting us because she had just given birth to our daughter. When we heard about a free seminar for a home-based business we took the opportunity to attend and find out if that was an option that would allow her to contribute to our income but stay home with our baby. This particular one had two different business opportunities available. One was owning gumball machines, which are considered silent sales. You placed the gumball machines in prime locations, maintained them on a periodic basis, and collected the proceeds. The second opportunity was selling distressed merchandise. If you're scratching your head wondering what that is, I understand because I did the same thing when I first heard about it.

Distressed merchandise is stuff that a manufacturer wants to get rid of for one reason or another. It is new merchandise, but it may be last year's model. It could be an overstock that the manufacturer has to get rid of prior to inventory or to make room for other products. Sometimes it is stuff that a manufacturer is discontinuing. Distressed merchandise can usually be purchased at deep discounts, sometimes up to 70 % off what the manufacturer normally charges for it. These are great bargains, but there are two main problems. The first problem is finding the merchandise. It is hard to know when a manufacturer is going to declare something as distressed so that they can get rid of it. The second problem with distressed merchandise is that the manufacturer usually wants to sell this stuff in lots or in case quantity, which means the end user is probably not going to be interested. Most people would not buy a pallet load of VCR's even if they could get them for $30 each instead of $90 each.

This outfit solved those two problems by acting as the middleman. They found the manufacturers with the distressed merchandise, and made the deal for the large lot quantity purchase. Then, they would fax their distributors the information on what was available, how many there were, and what the price and shipping charges were for each item. All the distributor had to do was determine what their markup was going to be and find the people who wanted to buy the item at that price.

I have said very little about the gumball machines, so you can imagine which home-based business opportunity Mary and I bought into. I didn't know how much of an effort it was going to be to try and sell something at give-away prices. I had hoped that Mary would put an effort into the business, since she was the one at home. Instead, I found myself putting all the work into it because Mary wasn't interested. We needed a business license, which was fairly easy to obtain downtown, and we needed business cards and stationary. Mainly we needed a way to receive the faxed opportunities from the company, and a way to distribute that information to our customers. I bought a computer with a fax modem, and soon figured out how to receive the faxes into the computer, edit them as I wanted and send them out to a group of clients. Every morning before I left for my job, I would look at the fax we'd received overnight. I'd cut and paste the pertinent information into a document with our sell price and our contact information, and I would fax it out to a small list of potential customers. We obtained the customer list from the Chamber of Commerce, and of course we put on each fax that if they wished to not be contacted they could call and be removed from the list. We started with over 300 companies that we faxed to, asking them to simply post the information near the time clock or in the employee cafeteria if they had one. Within a week, over a hundred and fifty companies had called us, not with merchandise orders, but to ask to be removed from the list. Within a month, we were down to about thirty companies that still received the fax from us. Whether those posted the advertisements or not I have no idea. They could have been unceremoniously dropping them into the garbage everyday. By this time we were involved in the training that the company provided for it's new distributors, hoping that it would give us the edge to make some sales.

The training was expensive, and it was a waste of time. Instead of providing solid leads, or showing how successful distributors were marketing themselves, they were merely trying to motivate me to "try something new" or to "consider new ways of distribution." I'd have gotten the same results from reading a self-help book at the library, and it would have been cheaper, too. I tried new tactics, like trying to sell to small family owned shops at a deeper discount, hoping to make it up in volume. Still, the phone didn't ring and the orders didn't pour in. Then I realized something I hadn't thought of before. Out of probably five thousand people who had attended the seminar, if only 1% of those people had gotten involved as I did, that meant that there were fifty other people out trying to do the same thing I was. Some of them probably could devote 30 hours a week to it. I was lucky if I had ten hours a week to put in after my hours at my job. I also started thinking that there was a problem with the way the business worked. I was trying to get people to prepay their orders, since the merchandise was non-returnable. I thought most people would not want to prepay for something they couldn't put their hands on from a company they'd never heard of before who was faxing the order form to them. I didn't even have a regular catalog, because the merchandise was never available for any length of time and it was always changing.

I decided to take a gamble and try something different. My sales were nonexistent, so I decided to purchase a few selected items, which I would have as my inventory, and I would try to sell those items at the flea market in town. I bought a collection of porcelain clown dolls that were very decorative and cost me about $1.09 each. I bought some glass jars with potpourri in them for $1.50 each. I bought some kids coloring books for a quarter each. The dolls were supposed to be selling at a retail price of $2.99 each, so I figured $1.75 was a good selling price. The potpourri should have gone for $3.59 in stores. The coloring books were worth about a dollar each. I was ready to start making some money, but I still didn't know all the details I needed.

When the dolls arrived I found that the exact same dolls could be purchased at two dozen stores in town for 99 cents each. The potpourri must have been last years inventory, because it was hardly fragrant at all. The coloring books were defects, which meant that instead of thirty some different pictures per book, each book had the same four pictures repeated eight times because of the way they had been bound. I had hardly anything I could sell, nothing I could return, and what I could sell I would have to take a loss on in order to get rid of it.

There were a lot of clowns given to my nieces that year for Christmas, and they each got some coloring books too. I gave up the idea of running this particular home-based business because I didn't have the time to devote to it, and I learned that you can't get someone else to be an entrepreneur if they aren't interested. Perhaps some of the other people who joined at the same seminar succeeded in making a go of it. I didn't because I didn't have the time to put in, and it seemed like an uphill battle.

I do know that I should have gotten more information before I got involved, and it was quite an expensive lesson to learn. There are a lot of legitimate home-based businesses out there, and there are a lot of scams. I know to avoid the get-rich-quick schemes and envelope-stuffing ones, because they are losing propositions. The opportunities that sound like they are feasible however, should really be researched before you get involved. There are hundreds of thousands of new companies formed each year, and about 80 % of them fail within two years. Most of them fail because they didn't get the details. They don't know if there is a market for their product or service. They haven't checked to see if their prices are competitive. They haven't learned what it takes to operate a business. Whether a person gets involved in a home-based business through a seminar like I did or they start up on their own, they should get the details of the business before they get involved, otherwise they will not be successful at it. I am not saying that home-based businesses cannot be successful, but they should not be gotten into on a whim.

Sleep on it before you sign

Years have passed since Mary and I divorced, and I remember the lesson I learned about home-based businesses, but what I should have learned from that episode was to take time to think before you make any decision that is going to cost you money. My fiancee, Chrystel, and I went to a meeting for ownership in a timeshare. Normally I have no interest in these things. I had just enough knowledge about how timeshares work to tell me that I didn't want to get involved, but occasionally I have subjected myself to sitting through a meeting just to get the door prize they offer. For this particular outfit, they were offering both a free digital camera and a three-night stay in a hotel in a "vacation destination." Chrystel had wanted a digital camera, and we decided it would be worth an hour or two of our time to go and listen to their sales pitch.

They held the meeting at one of their resort properties in our town, which was not only convenient but also showed that the properties were real. I have been to one or two of these meetings in the past where they have you meet in some hotel conference room they have rented. They show slide pictures of the properties but have nothing substantial. When you start asking for specific addresses of the resort locations they look at you strangely and dismiss you quickly. The meeting Chrystel and I attended was quite a bit better than that. They did have the slides, but at least we got to see firsthand the quality of the resort.

Most of the timeshare meetings I have sat through give you the typical formula. You purchase a week, for some it is always the same week each year and for others it's flexible, but you only get a week. You purchase certain sized accommodations and that is the size you will always have. If your family gets smaller because the kids grew up and moved out, you still get the same size. When you're taking a vacation with your in-laws and could use a bigger space, you can't get it unless you can find someone willing to trade. There are many problems with the traditional timeshares. That is why I avoided buying into one.

This one was different. It was a point-based timeshare, where you bought a certain number of points. If you needed a week in a one bedroom, it would be deducted from your points for the year. A weekend stay in a two bedroom required a different number of points, and that would be deducted from the points you had for the year. They had over fifty resorts that they owned that you could use your points in. Everything sounded really flexible. You could borrow points, save points, all within their rules, and you could have the kind of vacations you always dreamed about, the kind of vacations you deserved. That's what they said anyway.

It was an investment, something that we could even pass on to our children. They were building new resorts each year. Everything sounded fantastic. For as little as ten percent down they would even finance the rest. Chrystel and I looked at each other, talked about it some, and agreed to do it.

They give you every reason in the world why you have to make a decision that night. They may not be able to hold the price is one of the excuses. They are willing to waive some fee is another one. For us it was a combination of waiving some fees and we had to decide then if we wanted to become Premium owners. The Premium owners get lifetime ownership in the resorts, as long as all dues owed are paid of course, where a standard ownership expires after forty years. I guess it was late in the evening, because I didn't stop and think about how an ownership in something could expire because a certain number of years had gone by. Either you're an owner or you're not I would figure, but somehow they have it that the standard owners aren't owners after forty years. At lot of these timeshares are marketed toward retired people, so I guess some figure they don't need to worry about their ownership ending in forty years because they aren't likely to see it anyway.

Chrystel and I did talk about it before we signed, but we really didn't think about it. Not the kind of deep thinking an investment of money like this should involve. We should have told them that we would only purchase if we'd had a week to think about it and to read through the material to see if it was really right for us. This is not the way they want it to work, though, because they want your money. These types of businesses know that if you walk away without buying, chances are probably 99.9 % that you won't buy. They don't want to give you time to think about it.

I am not saying that Chrystel and I wasted our money, or that we made a bad decision, but we did make a rash one. We will pay over $1,800 a year for the next seven years to buy our ownership in the resorts. We will also pay an additional $400 or more per year for the maintenance dues for the rest of the time we are owners. If you figure this on a calculator, that's $12,600 for the ownership, and if we keep it for forty years that is $16,000 for forty years worth of maintenance dues. That $16,000 is if they don't raise the maintenance dues every year or so, which they can do. So, for forty years worth of ownership in the resorts, that is $28,600, or an average of $715 a year. For our average of $715 a year we get one week in a resort each year. That actually sounds better than saying I am paying $2,200 a year for the next seven years and then $400 a year for the next thirty three years after that.

We have put a lot of money into this timeshare, and there are times when we look at what we really get for our money and we think that maybe we shouldn't have done it. There are times when I look at my twenty year old truck that needs replaced and I think about how much money I am investing into our vacation timeshare that could have gone toward a newer vehicle. If I could go back in time to talk to myself sitting at that meeting, I wonder if I would tell myself to sign up. In ten years I might have a different answer than I do today.

No one should ever make a decision regarding something like this without having some time to think about it. A lot of these companies prey on people to make their money. They give you all the details, of course, but they present them so quickly and then they find ways to distract you from thinking about the details. I am not saying that these are not legitimate businesses, because most of them are, but they know how to high pressure you without making it seem like they are. If it is a good deal, you should be able to get materials from them that you can take home and read through, to talk to other people about, and then get back to them on your decision. There is nothing wrong with taking time to think about whether something like this is right for you or not, but they will make it seem like there is something wrong with you if you can't make a decision that night. Don't fall for this or any of their other tactics. Remember, they want your hard-earned money, and that is really the core of their business when you get right down to it. Before you sign your name on the contract, you should have time to see if it is right for you. If the deal is right, whatever it is, I am sure they will be just as happy to take your money a couple of days or a week later.

Chrystel and I haven't used our free digital camera in a while. You can't expect much quality in free electronics. We took our three-night complementary hotel stay in beautiful San Diego. The hotel was no resort, but it was safe and practical and conveniently located to everything we wanted to see and I'd recommend it to a friend. I'd also tell that friend how we got the free room. I'd tell them, when the telephone rings and you get invited to one of these meetings, it might be worth the hour or two of time you'll invest to get the "free" gift, but don't make a decision until you've had time to sleep on it.

Listen to the advice of others

My sisters both tried to warn me about getting involved with Mary. I was twenty-one at the time, and she was only seventeen. My sisters, Lynn and Kay, both knew that the chance of Mary and I staying together was pretty slim. The age difference wasn't the only thing. I was much more mature, and they knew Mary wasn't. I had a strong work ethic, and Mary had never held a job, and wasn't likely to. Intellectually we differed, and that can cause a great amount of problems in a relationship. I know all about the differences between us now, because I am older, and I am not in the relationship anymore, but at the time I could not see the differences and the problems they would make. I could not see them because I didn't want to see them. I was in love, and I didn't care what anyone else had to say.

Part of the reason I didn't want to listen to either of my sisters was because they were so close to my own age that I knew they didn't have much more experience at relationships than I did. I chose not to listen because I figured they didn't know what they were talking about. My dad gave very little advice, because that was his way, and Dad was usually one to let us make our own mistakes. After all, I was an adult, and I was far from stupid intellectually, so I should have been okay. The problem is, I was being stupid, because I did not seek out the advice of people who had been around, who might have steered me in the right direction. I was following my heart, and my brain was on auto-pilot.

My mother didn't offer her advice until later, because she knew me and knew I wasn't going to listen anyway. Mom saw the pattern I was in and understood that even if she talked to me about it, it was not advice I was apt to listen to. So, regardless of what everyone else thought, I went ahead and did what I wanted. Mary got pregnant, we got married, and a year-and-a-half after my daughter was born Mary left, saying she didn't want to be a wife and a mother anymore. I got custody of my daughter, and should have learned my lesson then, but I was still young and still did things my way.

During the eight months between when Mary left and I got involved with Cindy, the divorce went through and I moved into a new house. I had custody of my daughter, and things were okay but I wanted to be in a relationship, so I got involved with Cindy without really thinking things through. Again, I refused to heed the advice of the people around me. Now I had people at work even suggesting that Cindy and I shouldn't get married, because they could see what she was like and I wouldn't. My friend Chrystel tried to tell me that Cindy didn't really care about my daughter and I. Cindy wanted to get married, have the dress, the cake, the ceremony, and Chrystel could see that Cindy was only considering herself and her fantasy of being married. Cindy didn't want the reality of being in a relationship. Chrystel saw this and one night tried to warn me, but I flatly refused to listen and even told Chrystel that I was marrying Cindy and anyone that interfered could leave me alone and I wouldn't consider them to be a friend anymore.

I had closed my eyes again, so I wouldn't see the problems between Cindy and I. The differences between us didn't matter, or so I wanted to believe. So I refused to hear any advice other people tried to give me, and I married her in October of 1998. Our divorce was finalized in May of 2001. When I got involved with a woman named Gina following my second divorce, I had her living with me before I asked anyone's advice. My boss at work sat down with me and we talked about how things were at home, how Gina was treating my daughter, and about the situation I had gotten myself into. He told me that ultimately it was my decision, but he gave me his advice about the relationship. The relationship with Gina was a nightmare, and I have devoted an entire chapter to it, but in the end I took my bosses advice into consideration when I made my decision to ask Gina to move out. The relationship was doomed, and it was best to end it right then before too much more time went on.

Now I am involved with Chrystel, the girl who once tried to help me see what Cindy was like. I've talked to my family about her, to see how they feel about her. She has gotten to know my coworkers, and I occasionally consult with them regarding our relationship. This time around, I have found someone who everyone approves of, and they all believe Chrystel and I have a great shot at a lifelong, great relationship. Neither of us expects perfection, and we have a lot of similarities between us that give us a good foundation for our relationship. Both of us seem to understand that we occasionally need to listen to the advice of others regarding our relationship. She has her people that she talks to, and I have mine. I have learned that it is important to consider other people's advice in a lot of things, because we can benefit from an outside opinion or from someone else's experience.

When we are young, we think we know it all and can do it all, and we don't want to listen. I know I didn't, and I paid the price and in many ways my daughter paid the price with me. I didn't listen when someone told me I was involved with the wrong person. I didn't want to hear anything that went against the decisions I had made. Like my boss once said, ultimately the decisions we make are our own. No one else can make them for us, but we can make better decisions when we open ourselves to what others may have to say. Listening to the advice of others can benefit you in so many ways if you do it right. The first thing is to get more than one opinion, so that you can weigh the advice and see if it has merit. Sometimes one person's advice will conflict with someone else's, and that is when you will need to seek out more information. The main thing is to not be afraid of seeking advice. Don't allow yourself to be so stubborn that you don't listen. I made a lot more bad decisions when I didn't listen than when I did. The advice of someone who has been there, or who can see things from a different angle, can help you make the right decisions in your life as well. That is one of the main reasons I have written this book, so that maybe you will take my advice, and your life will be better because of it.

It sounds too good to be true

Chrystel needed some extra income, but she had a sporadic schedule at work to deal with, and it made it difficult to pick up anything else as a part time job. She also knew that if she took anything, it would mean less time to spend with me and with my daughter. I knew she didn't want to take a typical part time job, so I was not too surprised when she told me she had sent away for information about stuffing envelopes. What did surprise me was that Chrystel would have responded to one of those types of advertisements in the first place.

You know the kind of ads I am talking about. Some of them read 'Work from Home – Part Time – Earn Up to $4,000 a month' or 'Make Extra $$$ at Home.' There are a thousand different ways that people will try to get rich quick with little effort, and for each of those thousand ways, there are a thousand people trying to separate you from your money because of your desire to get rich without working for it.

The one Chrystel got hooked by said she could earn extra money by stuffing envelopes, and all she had to do was send a self-addressed stamped envelope along with $35 to find out how to do it. I tried to convince Chrystel that it was not going to be something she was willing to do, before she sent away her money, but she thought she'd try it because the information she had promised a money back guarantee. Her $35 went in the mail to them, and in a short period of time she got back her packet of information telling her how to make money by stuffing envelopes. Maybe you've figured how this one works yourself. Chrystel was supposed to place advertisements like the one she had responded to, telling people that they could make money by stuffing envelopes. Then, when they responded to her, she kept the $35 they sent and she mailed them a packet identical to the one she had received. They had no product, and they were not providing a service like putting circular ads into mailers for a company. The people who had been conned into sending in $35 were supposed to perpetuate the con on other people. If Chrystel conned ten people a month with her ads, she grossed $350, but she had to pay to place the ads and to photocopy the information packet however many times, and that was supposed to provide her with an income. Chrystel couldn't do it. She is too good-natured to scam people that way. As for the money-back guarantee, she would have had to actually put advertisements in newspapers and such so many times before they were willing to give her back her money, and she didn't want to, so she accepted that she'd been conned and that was the end of it.

There are tons of deals like this out there, and while some are legitimate business opportunities most of them are just fluff designed to separate you from your hard-earned money. The government has designed rules against multi-level marketing and pyramid schemes, where the people who recruit you form one level, you are a level, and you have to recruit people and they recruit to form the levels below you. These types of schemes are illegal, but the government left enough wiggle room in the laws that there are still some companies that exist with similar setups that vary just enough to squeak by the law. The problem with these is that they are rarely moneymakers, despite what you are shown in a seminar.

For my parents, it was Amway. Amway started off selling laundry soaps and cleaners, and after a few years you could find just about anything in the Amway catalog. My dad says that Amway made great laundry soap, and they would contract with other companies on the other products they sold so the pricing wasn't too bad, and the quality was good, but the products weren't the problem. The problem with Amway all those years ago was having to constantly hold meetings in your house or at someone else's house to recruit more people, to keep the whole thing propped up by having enough people under you buying so you got your cut. I can't give you the whole story on Amway, and I know some people made money, but most just found the whole thing to be a hassle not worth their time and money.

Amway wasn't the only one out there, but they are probably one of the more recognizable names. I remember one long-distance phone company that I belonged to that wanted me to hold meetings in my home to recruit more long-distance customers for them, and I would get a percentage of all the long-distance call charges made by the people I recruited. I believe that company is now out of business as a result of a government investigation. I don't know if the government ever decided the company was doing something illegal, but they created enough of a problem for the company that they had to close.

Just two years ago, I got a call from Dale, my former boss. It had been eight years since I had quit working for Dale, and he had gone back to teaching high school. He asked me if I could come to dinner to discuss a business opportunity. I told him I'd come because I hadn't seen him in a long time, and if nothing else I would get a free dinner out of it. Dale wasn't alone for the dinner, he'd brought along someone above him to help explain the deal, since Dale was in training. They talked about teaching people to change their buying habits, so that I could make a percentage off what the people were going to buy. They talked about the convenience of online shopping, and how we weren't going to try to sell something people didn't need, we were just going to teach them to buy from our online store and enjoy the convenience. After a half-hour of listening to them talk about this stuff, I asked what the product was. I got fifteen minutes of simple examples, of how it was basic stuff that people needed to buy anyway, that they generally were not buying on impulse. They talked about how these products were ones that people used everyday, and they knew when they were starting to run out and they could order from my online store, and have it delivered conveniently in a few days right to their door. I asked again what the products were. They started talking about shampoo and conditioner and then they mentioned laundry soap. I sort of laughed and said something about Amway. By this time they had pulled out a product flyer illustrating the items they had for sale. Whoever had put the sale flyer together had done a really good job with the text, because no where on that flyer was the Amway name ever printed, but in the glossy pictures of the products, larger than life, I could read the Amway name on the boxes.

They are still out there, and they are still trying to recruit, and I knew I didn't want to have anything to do with it. I told Dale I appreciated the dinner, but I had a kid to raise and a full time job as well, and I didn't have time to be having meetings and recruiting people to buy and sell Amway products. Apparently Dale later decided it wasn't for him either, because several months later I talked to him and he'd given it up too. He had decided he needed to spend time with his family, not traveling all over the city trying to get people to buy into the dream of getting rich quickly because of the efforts of people beneath you in the pyramid.

Like I said, there are real opportunities out there, and some people can and do make money in these things. For most people, though, it will never happen. In the meeting they make it sound so easy, like people are just waiting to step in line behind you and help propel you toward wealth. In the advertisements, they make it sound like you can make a lot of money for almost no work, like it is something you can do while your feet are propped up and you're watching television. Some of these things are illegal, and are just operating long enough to rake in a couple of thousand dollars for their operators from unsuspecting people before they close down to avoid detection by the government. Others, like the envelope stuffing may be legal but they certainly border on being ethical. Chrystel and I know we couldn't collect money from other people like that. Amway and ones like them in the world don't tell you how hard you'd really have to work, and how many people you'll alienate along the way, if you were to truly succeed in their businesses. Usually it comes down to the old axiom, about how if something sounds too good to be true, it probably is. These get rich quick schemes all sound too good to be true. They promise wealth can be attained with little or no work. Usually that won't happen. Usually, these schemes are lots of work and little reward. Usually, they aren't worth getting involved in, because they sound too good to be true, and they are.

Watch out for scams

I wanted to talk about how important it is to watch out for scams, but I couldn't draw from my own personal experience on this topic. However, I can tell you what happened to my sister.

My sister was using America Online for her internet access, and it was billed to her debit card on her checking account. She received an email that informed her that they needed to confirm her credit card information within 48 hours or her internet access would be canceled. My sister thought this was a bit unusual, so she tried to contact AOL's billing department by phone. She couldn't get through that night. She tried sending an email reply to the message, but got no response. The following night she decided, because she didn't want to lose her internet access, to fill out the form contained in the email and she gave them her debit card number and expiration date.

It wasn't too many days later that she found her checking account balance was off. She checked with the bank and found four transactions that she had not made, all billed to her debit card. The charges had drained her account to the point that she was hit with a couple non-sufficient fund fees. The account was frozen when my sister notified the bank, so that no more charges could be made, and she was issued a new account number. Fortunately, the money was refunded and she was not liable for the amounts charged by whomever had pulled the scam on her. Unfortunately, she had a major hassle regarding some of the checks she had written which were returned for insufficient funds, and she had to argue with a couple of companies to get late fees taken off her bills.

Most banks and credit unions nowadays have policies that protect the consumer from fraudulent scams and credit card theft like my sister experienced, but it is still a headache to deal with. Also, depending on whether you are using a debit card or a credit card, your liability can vary. My sister was refunded all of the money that she was out, but I know she spent several hours on the phone trying to straighten things out. She was without a debit card for several days until the bank got a replacement to her, but after a couple of weeks things were pretty much back to normal for her.

When I finally talked to my sister about what had happened to her, she showed me a printout of the original email she had received. It looked pretty official, but I reminded her that AOL and most of the other internet service providers have policies that they cannot ask you for your credit card or password information by email. I also pointed out to her that the email address looked phony, because it did not originate from AOL. In an email address, there are two parts. The first part is the user name, and the second is the domain name. It looks like user@domain.name. If the email had come from AOL, it most likely would have had @aol.com as the domain, and this particular email did not. My sister told me she had been suspicious about it, but she had gone ahead and replied anyway because she was not certain if it was legitimate or not.

My sister responded, even though there were clues that this was a scam. Regardless of how intelligent she is, she fell for a pretty simple trap. I doubt that she was the only one. Crimes like this occur frequently, because it is difficult to catch the perpetrators. If only ten people responded to this bogus email like my sister did, the crooks who did it probably got away with five to six thousand dollars worth of stuff billed against the innocent. Like I said, my sister was refunded, which was a relief to her. For some credit card theft, you can be held responsible for the first

$50 billed against you. I have heard that in some cases on a debit card you can be held responsible for the first $500. In either case, this is a huge hassle that everyone should want to avoid.

If you're online, use extreme caution in giving out your debit or credit card information. Don't respond to requests for your information from an unsolicited email. In stores, take your receipts with you. Most credit card machines nowadays obliterate or disguise your account number on the printed receipt, but that is not always the case. Keep your receipts for all your credit card charges and compare them against your monthly statement. If anything is amiss, contact the credit card company and request proof that the charge was legitimate. For your debit card that is attached to your checking account, make sure you keep the register up-to-date and balance the account every month.

If you find that you have been scammed, contact the bank, credit union, or credit card company immediately. They can help you straighten things out, and the better prepared you are the less of a headache you'll have in getting things put right. If you can't tell them what charges you made because you didn't keep receipts or write anything down, it will be difficult to fix the problem. Some people may not even realize they've been scammed for a couple of months because they don't compare their credit card statements monthly against their receipts. You don't have to be one of these disorganized people. Keep your checking and credit accounts up-to-date, or you'll have a hard time telling what your balance should have been. Be cautious with who you give credit and debit card numbers to. Being cautious is not a guarantee that somewhere along the way you won't be scammed, but it will cut down on your chances.

Protect your identity

I recently got my eyes examined for new eyeglasses. While I was waiting, I had the usual form to fill out, and I came to the spot where they asked for a social security number. I was reminded how much our lives revolve around that little number, and how little we think of it.

Our social security numbers were never meant to be used for identification except by the government, and now they are used everywhere. In most states, your social security number is used as your drivers license number, although some states allow you to request otherwise. But states are not the only ones that use this number to identify who we are. Credit card companies use it to link us to all the places we borrow money from. The credit reporting agencies use the number to keep track of late payments, over credit limit balances, payment histories, and a whole lot of other information that most people don't understand and rarely give thought to. Health insurance companies use it as our identification number. The number is now used so prolifically that it is almost impossible to keep it private.

I have seen social security numbers asked for on paperwork I had to fill out for my daughter's school. It's not that they are required to make sure they are educating only citizens of our country, because they laws around here are such that they can't deny an education to anyone whether they are a citizen or not. I could figure no reason why they would need it. It is on applications for renting videos from certain chain stores. I would think it would be enough that they have my debit card information to bill me if I don't return a video, but they want the social security number, too. Maybe they are going to report non-returned videos like late payments on my credit report. My auto insurance carrier has my number, because they are now using my credit report to gauge how likely I am to file a claim, and that is how they are setting my insurance premiums. My employer needs the number, so they can report taxes to the federal government, but elsewhere it is sometimes hard to see why some companies need the information.

That is where the biggest problem comes about. When we hear of identity theft, it is not someone impersonating another to get a job. I don't think anyone has ever stolen another person's identity so they could pay the other's traffic tickets or do jail time for them. Identity theft is when one person uses another person's information to open credit card charge accounts, which they then use to buy things fraudulently. Since most people don't check their credit reports very often, it often goes unnoticed for a while, until the collectors start calling wanting their money for the things they think we bought.

The problem grows each time we let another company use our social security number to identify us. Every piece of paper that we fill out with that information could be accessed by someone savvy enough to use it to open a credit card account in our name. We have to find another way, a means of identifying ourselves that is not tied to opening credit accounts. Until there is a way of doing this that is not related to debts to repay, then we make ourselves targets for the criminal element.

We now live in a world where we have little privacy. What we need to do is take back some of that privacy. Anytime you are asked to provide your social security number, you should have a light go off in your head, and maybe you should hear a bell ringing, too. You need to ask why they need that information. You need to find out who has access to it, and you need to ask if they can use another means to identify you. This is not foolproof, but it will reduce your chances of someone getting your social security number and doing something fraudulent with it. It is your responsibility to protect your identity as best you can so you won't have problems later.

Follow directions

On Father's Day in the year 2000, I figured I would catch up on some much-needed projects around my house. I was married to Cindy at the time, and she was at work, so it was just my daughter and I at the house. I left my daughter inside watching Disney movies, and I headed outside. I started off with repainting some trim work around the house, using a six-foot-tall stepladder. I spent the better part of the morning working on the house, sweating in the June sun. I know most guys would see Father's day as a day of rest, a day to get away from the work around the house, but I was enjoying myself and I was getting quite a lot done. The house certainly looked better when I was done with it, and then I moved on to repainting around my storage shed. I have a great shed in the back yard, it's made of cement block and is painted to match the house. The shed is part of the reason I bought the house, because the last place I'd lived I'd had a weather-beaten dented tin shed that leaked water when it rained and was not a secure place for anything. My shed at the house is built to last.

The work was going fine, even though the stepladder was too short to reach everywhere I needed to. I found myself standing on the very top of it, above the spot marked "Do not stand above this line." I finished the painting and decided that I would trim the tree that is just outside of my shed. The tree is close enough to the shed that if I let it grow and don't keep it trimmed, it's branches will scrape against the wood trim on the shed, and that is why I had to repaint the shed in the first place. I put my painting equipment up and got out the tree saw, intending to finish up my work by trimming the tree and calling it a day. I had already accomplished a lot, and I wanted to relax some in the afternoon because there was a barbecue planned at my sister's house in the evening.

Now almost done with trimming the tree, I repositioned the ladder to get at another branch. I climbed back up and stood, again, on the very top of the stepladder. I reached up to take hold of the branch, and must have over-extended my reach, because the ladder shifted beneath me. I looked down, and saw it rock up on two of its four feet, and then it toppled. In the space of a second, I fell. I somehow shifted my weight, trying to jump clear of the ladder, but I came down on top of it instead. I put my hand down instinctively, trying to break my fall. I landed, with my arm stretched down and my hand open, and landed on my back, with the ladder under me. I am sure I cried out, and probably uttered some profanity as well. I rolled over, off the ladder, and got myself into a sitting position. Gravel was embedded in my skin, and I was sweating as if someone had turned on a water faucet. I looked down at my right arm, and saw a peculiar sight. My arm was still straight, but at my wrist my hand was offset by about an inch, as a road might jog over and then go straight again. I knew immediately that it was broken. It was the first time in my life I'd ever broken anything in my body.

I went back into the house, my arm in severe pain, and my daughter called over to my dad's house. My daughter was only five years old at the time, and she did a fantastic job of dialing the phone correctly on the first try, considering her father was now sitting on the kitchen floor dripping in sweat and wincing at the pain in his arm. Fortunately, my dad lives just a half-mile away, and my sister was there and she arrived at my door minutes later.

There is more to the story, like having to sit in the hospital for three hours before I got my arm cast so I could leave.

There is the part about how they administered morphine for the pain, and that was when it was discovered that I have an allergic reaction to morphine. There's the part about how a team of doctors debated on whether they needed to perform surgery and pin the bone in place or if a cast would suffice. There was the reaction I got when I walked into work on Monday morning wearing a cast. The story goes on with having to have physical therapy to stretch the tendons and rebuild the muscles in my arm and wrist. I also discovered a year and a half later that when I landed on my back on top of the ladder, I damaged my back, and I am not sure if it will ever be right again. While there is so much more to this story than I have told you, I have told you enough that you can see the trouble I got into by not following directions.

We all take a lot of risks in life. Sometimes we come out lucky. Sometimes we don't. I knew it was dangerous to stand on top of a stepladder, but it was the only ladder I had at the time. I justified the risk in my mind because I had done the same thing before, and I had not had a problem. Life is full of risks, and sometimes we want to take them, because that broadens our horizons and makes us feel alive. To sit in a safe environment all the time and never take chances limits our experiences, but we have to be prepared for the consequences of taking chances. There are times when you should take risks, and there are times when you should play it safe. I know on ladders now, I choose to play it safe. I bought a proper extension ladder after that incident, because breaking an arm is not something I consider fun.

It may be difficult to know when to play it safe. When you might injure someone other than yourself, then you should play it safe. There are enough troubles in this world without being a danger to someone else. If you are the only person who could be injured by your actions, then you may decide the risk is acceptable. You may want to minimize your chances of injury however, by doing whatever is necessary to make the activity safer. Jumping out of an airplane when you've been trained and have the right equipment is safer than if you did it without training and with a homemade parachute. Your chances of living a long, healthy life are greater if you follow directions. If you need training, get it. If you need the right equipment, buy it. If you need advice, ask.

Check your credit report

I have learned now that it is better to avoid going into debt, but there is a time when most people need to borrow money even if they can manage to pay cash for everything else. That time comes when you buy a house. This is one time when having a good credit report is extremely important. The first place I bought to live was an old single-wide trailer. I borrowed money on my credit card for a down payment and the owner carried the rest. There was no real qualifying and I wasn't shopping around for the lowest mortgage interest rate I could get, so I didn't learn then how important your credit report is. I learned that lesson when I bought my house.

My first wife, Mary, had been in a vehicle accident when she was seventeen. Because she had been a minor, her parents were responsible for her medical bills, which of course they couldn't pay. They filed a lawsuit, which took a couple of years to settle. Once she turned eighteen and legally became an adult, Mary also became a party to the lawsuit, since she was the one injured. When we got married, I also became a party to the lawsuit because of the laws of our state. The lawsuit finally settled and the hospitals were paid what they agreed to settle for. Mary and I used half the money to pay off our bills and the other half we put as a down payment on a house. Since we had to finance the house, the mortgage company pulled a copy of both of our credit reports.

I didn't think there would be any real problem with them doing this, since we had just paid everything off. I had rarely been late making payments, even when I'd been in debt on the credit cards. Sometimes I'd only been able to pay minimum payments, but that is actually looked on favorably since the bank gets to make more money the longer you stretch out repaying them. Most of the accounts had been closed anyway, so there was nothing I was concerned about. Then the lender told us there were many items on my credit report from the hospital and the doctors showing that Mary's medical bills were my responsibility. The report said payments had not been made and that balances had been turned in for collections. The balances now showed paid, but the remarks about the late payments and the collections were very much against us. The lender told us that if we were lucky they would be able to get us an interest rate around 10 % instead of the 7 % rate that we could have gotten if our credit hadn't been a mess. I learned then that even with the hospital having been paid the money that was due to them, once something is put on your credit report it can drastically affect you. Companies that you owe money to can put derogatory information in your credit report as long as it is accurate, and that information will be there for years even if you catch up or pay off the balance. If you are constantly late making payments, that information will affect you in the future. If you have ever been sent to collections, that is terrible information that will be on your credit report. Even if you have managed your credit and have not been behind on payments or been sent to collections, it is still very important to check your credit report to make sure there aren't any errors there.

I managed to get my credit report cleaned up of the remarks by the hospitals and the doctors. I contacted the lawyer who had filed the lawsuit, and he contacted them. Since Mary had been a minor at the time the debts were incurred, her parents were the ones legally responsible for the hospital bills, and under state law they were still responsible for the debt even when she became an adult. He convinced them that Mary and I were never responsible. Since the information they had put in my credit report was inaccurate, they were forced to remove it within 30 days. We had to get the lender to hold off on the paperwork long enough to clear this up, and we received the lower interest rate. This saved me thousands of dollars, and taught me a very important lesson.

I didn't learn to manage my credit, but I did learn to get a copy of my credit report annually to review it for errors. If you want to buy anything on credit this is very important. Instead of getting the low interest rate you saw advertised on a car, you could end up paying a couple of percentage points higher because of the information in your credit report. The small amount you will pay for your credit report each year is insignificant compared to how much more money you can be charged if it has wrong information in it and you are borrowing money somewhere. Remember, you want to manage your money, and if you are buying on credit you have to manage your credit history as well. If you can't avoid being late or being sent to collections, only time will purge the negative information if it is true. Anything in there that is not true is up to you to clean up, and you can only do that if you know it's there.

When to keep your mouth shut

I met Raymond when we were in elementary school. We knew each other, but he was a year older and a grade above me, so we weren't really close friends until years later. In junior high we were hardly around each other at school, but in high school Raymond and I became best friends.

As best friends, Raymond and I did a lot of boring stuff together, like just hanging out and watching television when there was nothing else to do, but we did a lot of interesting things too. There was the time we got in trouble because he'd borrowed a truck without permission from his dad. He was 15 at the time and didn't have a driver's license. His dad bought and sold vehicles a lot, so there were generally more vehicles parked around their house than there were people to drive them. The one Raymond took, unfortunately, didn't have a license plate on it. Raymond drove for a little ways and then asked me where we should go. I suggested a direction that led us down a road that lead to a dead-end, and it happened that a cop was parked at the dead end that very day. We got pulled over by the cop and he threatened to haul us off to juvenile court. Instead we were turned over to Raymond's mom. Raymond had to work a lot to pay off the traffic ticket he got, but in the end the court was lenient with him. They could have prevented him from getting his license until he was eighteen but they didn't. Raymond never blamed me for getting caught even though I'd suggested the direction.

Another time, Raymond helped me win a stuffed elephant from an arcade. There was a popular place in town that had a game room in the building and a race track behind it where you could race miniature Indy 500 race cars. It was a cool place to hang out because they had all the familiar video games. Some games dispensed tickets depending on the score you got, and you could collect those tickets and turn them in for prizes. One of my favorite games was skee ball. If you had a decent score in skee ball, you got about five tickets, and a really good score could get you about eight tickets. I was trying to win a two-foot-tall stuffed gray elephant that you had to have about 1500 tickets to win. I wanted to win the elephant for a girl I was interested in, and Raymond helped me play skee ball games for about a month to win enough tickets to get it. I only went out with the girl twice. Raymond was the kind of friend who would help you out like that though, even if you were wasting your time.

We hung out together for a couple of years. When we were still in our teens, we were interested in cruising around town. Our idea of cruising was not just back and forth on the same street all the time like you would think of. To us, the whole town was ours to explore. We would head west where the houses were few and far between, where the sky was dark and you could actually see the stars overhead. We'd cruise over to the east side of town where there was a miniature golf course with an arcade room, bumper boats, and mini-race-cars. Raymond and I weren't much into hanging out at a club during those years, because we were to young to drink and were more interested in driving. We would put a hundred or more miles on a car in a single night, just enjoying driving around while the radio played and we talked about anything and everything and nothing. Mostly we talked about school and work, the things that occupied our time when we weren't driving.

We worked together at a restaurant for a couple of years, washing dishes and cleaning up at the end of the night. Often on the weekends after work we would head down to one of the local bowling alleys with a couple of other people from work. Even after Raymond graduated from high school the year before I did, we still spent a lot of time hanging out with each other.

I had a bad experience with a girl named Maggie when I was sixteen, so during the years when we were in high school together Raymond had a couple of girlfriends and I dated very rarely. I was interested in a couple of girls, of course, but I was wary of them at the same time. Sometimes Raymond, whatever girl he was dating at the time, and I would go out together to hang out, and rarely was it a problem that they were a couple and I was by myself. Occasionally I would feel like a extra wheel and I would go off to do my own thing. It would give them time to be together without me around. Raymond usually made time to hang out with me at least once a week anyway, so it wasn't like I was excluded. I tried to not interfere in Raymond's relationships, even when he was dating a girl from another school and he was skipping school constantly to go see her. I figured it was his business, and I said nothing, but there came a time when I did speak my mind.

After Raymond graduated from high school, he got involved with a girl named Danielle. She used to live in the neighborhood when we were all in elementary school, but she had moved away. Danielle had been friends with my sister years before, and she'd gotten back in touch with her. One of them suggested a night out with Danielle, Raymond, my sister and I going to the movies together. I think my sister wanted to date Raymond, and possibly for me to date Danielle, but Raymond was interested in Danielle and I wasn't. I was still in high school and Danielle was about nineteen years old and already had a son from some other guy.

It didn't take too long before Raymond and Danielle were officially dating. I saw how Raymond's attitude changed, about a lot of things. I knew he thought he loved her, but they didn't seem very happy together. It often seemed like he would try to manufacture happiness. I may be wrong, but that was my opinion. I suspected that Danielle was just looking for someone, anyone, to help her raise her kid. I didn't think she really cared about Raymond, that she was only using him. I told Raymond I didn't think Danielle was any good for him. I tried to talk to him, and instead he suspected that I was jealous, that I had wanted to be with Danielle myself and was trying to split them up, which was so far from the truth. I had no interest in her whatsoever, but he was my best friend and I thought that if I talked to him he might see for himself and could get out of the relationship before he really got hurt.

By telling Raymond what I thought of the woman he was with, Raymond turned on me. Our friendship ended right there, even though we still worked together at the restaurant. It got to where he wouldn't speak to me, and that was something I had to live with. He chose her and he didn't want to hear anything bad about her from me. It was his right to do so. They lived together for a few years, but never married as far as I know. They had two kids, plus her son that Raymond helped raise for a while. Why they finally split up after a couple years I don't know. Whether I had been right about Danielle at the beginning or not I am uncertain. All I know is that they lived together, produced a couple of kids together, and then went their separate ways.

There are times in your life when you have to speak up, regardless of what the consequences might be. You have to say something if you have a friend who is doing something destructive, like abusing drugs or alcohol. Interfering in a friend's relationship can be pretty tricky business, though. Raymond could have taken my advice and avoided Danielle, but maybe he had a couple good years with her, and he does have a couple of kids that he wouldn't have had otherwise. Regardless of whether I said anything or not, it was his business, and I probably should have stayed out of it. Sometimes you have to let other people make mistakes on their own. You have to learn to keep your mouth shut and let them live their lives without your interference. All you can do is just be there for them if they fail. Making mistakes proves we're human, and showing compassion for others when they make a mistake keeps us humane. If I'd kept my opinions to myself, I'd have kept a friend, and those are hard to come by.

Roommates from hell (part 1)

Roommates can be a lot of fun. They can also cost you a lot of money and a lot of grief. My old high school friend Raymond needed a place to live, and I had a spare bedroom. Raymond and Danielle were ancient history by this time, and we had started patching up our friendship so I rented the room out to him for $300 a month, utilities and basic cable included. He had access to laundry facilities and his own bathroom. We didn't write up a lease because despite our disagreements over Danielle, Raymond had always been trustworthy.

Raymond went out quite a bit, but I was just recently divorced from Mary and was raising my daughter pretty much by myself at that point, so I couldn't go out too often. Periodically though I would go out with Raymond and his friends, and they'd come over to hang out at my house. Raymond paid his rent regularly for the first six or seven months that he lived there, and everything was fine between us. Then Raymond went to Seattle on a road trip with his friends. He really couldn't afford it, but he went anyway. When he came back, he continued his lifestyle of going out to eat almost nightly. He wasn't dining at McDonald's either, he was going to Applebee's and other more expensive places where he could eat and drink and he routinely spent $30 to $40 a night. He started getting behind on his rent.

One month he paid me only $100, saying that he would get the rest to me in a couple of weeks. The next month he only paid $200, which put him $300 behind. Raymond started avoiding me because he couldn't pay his rent. He made sure he was out of the house before I woke up in the morning, and he wouldn't come back to the house until well after I had fallen asleep. He stayed another month like that, and occasionally I would see him and he would say he was going to have the money, and then I wouldn't see him for another week. When he was $600 behind in his rent, I confronted him. I had to ask him to move out of my house since he couldn't pay his rent.

I had nothing in writing, and I also learned that you are supposed to get permission from the local government to rent out a portion of your house like that, so I couldn't take Raymond to small claims court for what he owed me. I probably wouldn't have taken him to court anyway, since he had been my friend for so many years. I did quit talking to him however, and I haven't spoken to him since because I feel he took advantage of our friendship. He agreed to pay me for his rent and he never did pay what he owed. I should have gotten a written agreement about the rent, but more importantly I never should have had a friend as a roommate. Having a roommate not pay what they are supposed to is bad enough, but it is worse when it is a friend, and the situation puts a strain on the friendship. I did what I felt I needed to since Raymond wasn't paying what he'd agreed, but he stopped talking to me and I quit talking to him.

Fortunately Raymond didn't cost me any real money. He never paid me, but the money he had paid me had been a supplement to my income. He didn't leave me with any astronomically high utility bills and he didn't do any damage to my house that needed repaired. Raymond didn't cost me any money that had to come out of my pocket, but the whole situation cost me far more in the long run. It cost me a friend.

Roommates from hell (part 2)

I thought I was doing someone a favor. Not too much time had passed since I had told Raymond to move out of the room he was renting from me. Then the woman who was to be my second wife, Cindy, was living with my daughter and I. At this point, I'd had my fill of roommates, but Cindy asked if her best friend, Claire, could stay with us on a temporary basis. Claire had recently separated from her husband and had nowhere else to stay. We talked about it and I reluctantly agreed, and Claire moved in on the understanding that she was going to pay $100 a month to help cover utilities but that the arrangement was only temporary.

We didn't expect Claire to stay with us for too long. During the first month she was living with us, she helped with housework and doing the dishes, and even helped me with yard work. Cindy was usually working in the evenings, so Claire often made dinner and had it ready for when my daughter and I came home. It seemed like Claire was making every effort to repay us for letting her stay. Then, things changed and it seemed like Claire was trying to drive a wedge between Cindy and I.

When I was at home and Cindy was at work, Claire would tell me how terribly Cindy was treating my daughter. Claire even went so far as to suggest that I plant a camera in the house to record what went on when I was not around. Since I had seen no examples of the kind of behavior Claire talked about, I had a hard time believing her. I confronted Cindy, and she told me she would never treat my daughter that way. Then, Cindy asked me about how Claire was treating us. I told her about the dinners being made and Claire cleaning and helping around the house. Cindy felt Claire was flirting with me, and she said she had seen it herself. She thought that Claire was trying to convince me to dump her by saying she was mistreating my daughter. Cindy suggested that if Claire convinced me to break up with her, Claire would have a place to live and a new man in her life. I had no interest in Claire whatsoever, so I told her I didn't want to hear anything more about the things Cindy was supposedly doing. I told her I didn't want to have anything to do with her at all. Claire did quit talking about Cindy, but things were still pretty awkward around the house.

Claire started spending a lot of time by herself, surfing the internet while my daughter and I watched television, or she would be on the phone for hours. Most of the time this behavior didn't bother me since it seemed she was trying to not intrude too much into our lives anymore, and she was not disturbing my relationship with Cindy. After my daughter went to bed each evening, however, I often felt like Claire was taking too many liberties around the house. I could never use the telephone and could rarely get to my computer because Claire was on one or the other. Often I would watch television until about ten o'clock when Cindy got home, and we would go to bed while Claire remained on the computer or on the telephone until two or three in the morning. Often at night I could not sleep because I could hear Claire typing away as she visited the internet chat rooms. I was feeling real sorry that I had agreed to let Claire stay with us and she was not being respectful that it was not her house to just do as she pleased.

After about six weeks of Claire living with us, she moved out and went back to her husband. Things should have gotten back to normal, except a couple of days later, I got my telephone bill in the mail. Claire had been calling the psychic hotlines regularly, and my telephone bill was over $300 when it was normally only $29 a month. Claire refused to pay it, as well as the $100 she was supposed to pay for her rent. I pretty much came unglued. I told Cindy I never wanted Claire around my house again. That didn't exactly happen but Cindy did make sure she was never around my house again while I was there. The following month my telephone bill was over $140, plus the balance from the previous month. I called the telephone company and explained that my telephone had been used without my knowledge and without my permission. At first they did not want to credit the charges, but finally I spoke to a supervisor who agreed to credit the account most of the charges. I ended up paying only what my normal bill was plus about $40 of the charges Claire had made.

I got lucky that I didn't have to pay the full amount. Normally the telephone company will hold you responsible for something like that. After all, I had given Claire permission to use the phone, and I had never told her that she would be responsible to pay any unusual charges she made. Since I'd already had the experience of having Raymond live at my house and not pay his rent, I should have known to get something in writing with Claire but I didn't, and I paid for my mistake.

Put it in writing

I have heard how important it is to put things in writing, but I have not always lived by it. I should have with Raymond and Claire, but it probably wouldn't have mattered in either situation. When Dan conned me into signing over the legal rights to my Jeep before I had received payment for it, he signed a promissory note that he would pay me for the Jeep if he sold it. Since he disappeared with my money and I had no idea where he'd gone or how to track him down, the promissory note wasn't worth the paper it was written on. He probably knew that if he got far enough away I'd never be able to collect, because even if I did find him, it would cost me a lot of money just to attempt to collect.

When I sold my Dad a van and he didn't have the money to pay up front, I didn't need to write out anything, because I knew my Dad would pay it without question. That is the kind of guy my father is, and I knew I could trust him. I thought I could trust Raymond not to cheat me over money, because we had been such good friends for years, so I didn't put a rental agreement into writing with him. That time I should have, because he ended up not paying what he owed. Maybe if I'd had something in writing between us I'd have gotten paid.

About six months before Dan got his hands on the Jeep, the transmission had gone out of it and I didn't have the money to fix it, and I was desperate because I had no other transportation to get back-and-forth to work. Cliff, a guy from work, loaned me the money for the parts and helped me on Christmas Day to put it together in his garage, because that's the kind of guy he is. Cliff also is a guy who had learned from his past, because he won't loan money to just anyone, and he had me sign a promissory note to pay him back in a timely manner. I did, and that situation went well, although I doubt I'd ever repeat rebuilding a transmission on a Christmas Day. That's just not a way to spend a holiday.

I have seen on the small claims court shows regularly where one side presents their side and the other tells something totally opposite, but the one who has the paperwork usually prevails. It's not enough to come to an agreement anymore; you usually should put something in writing to at least describe what's supposed to happen. I know a lot of people go with prenuptial agreements before they get married, and that isn't always a bad idea, but in some ways I think that is almost like planning divorce from the start. If you actually build a lifelong relationship where you work out the troubles instead of abandoning ship, then the prenuptial agreement is unnecessary. Other than that, I think it's a good idea to write things down.

If you share an apartment with someone, put it in writing who is expected to pay what, or there will probably be a problem. If you loan someone more money than you can afford to lose without missing it, then you should write it down. You should do this to protect yourself not only from not being paid, but to put to rest claims that exceed what you agreed to. The other important thing about putting all this stuff in writing is to get it signed by the people involved, with witnesses if you suspect you need them. Then each person signing should get a copy.

One last thing that is extremely important to put in writing is instructions concerning your demise. Anything can and does happen, and if you have other people relying on you this is extremely important. You can decide for yourself if you need a will, a living trust, or whatever other options there may be, but have something written down. Let people know what you want done with your stuff, and if you have kids let the state know whom you have chosen as their guardian. There are options for setting up wills and such using computer software for relatively inexpensive costs, so there are no excuses for not doing it. Make the time, figure it out, and save your loved ones a lot of grief later. You can protect a lot of things in life and afterward, by putting things in writing.

Teenage sex

I was sixteen years old the first time I had sex. I was working weekends at a theme park near my house as part of the custodial crew. It wasn't bad work and at least I got to move around the park rather than being stuck in one location all day like the kids operating the rides. It also gave me a chance to interact with the other people who worked there. Most of the people who worked there on weekends were teenagers like myself, since the place only paid minimum wage. Being on the custodial crew meant I could visit the shops and talk to the cashiers, I could visit with the entertainment crew when they were between shows, and I could wander over to the rides area and talk to the people operating the attractions. The mobility was great because I got to meet so many of my co-workers while I did my own job. The only other position in the park that had as much mobility was security, but I was only sixteen and was not qualified for that job.

Maggie worked for the food crew, so she would be stationed in whichever restaurant or café needed someone for the day. My sister, Kay, also worked on the custodial crew with me, and she met Maggie and then introduced her to me. I started meeting her in the employee cafeteria for lunch every day, and we began dating outside of work a few weeks later. Since we were teenagers, and we were both working for minimum wage and only on weekends, our dates were usually pretty simple because they had to be inexpensive. I was driving a car that was almost thirty years old and I didn't have a car payment but I was paying for car insurance and the car was a gas guzzler, so there wasn't much money left to take a girl out. Usually we hung out at her house and watched movies, or we would go out to eat at a fast food joint. Being young and dumb, we slept together on several occasions.

After maybe two months, I had some reason for breaking up with Maggie, and I took her out to tell her I wanted to end our relationship. We went to different high schools, liked different things, and I got tired of Maggie expecting me to be around her constantly when I had little free time as it was. Instead of the evening being about regaining my freedom, however, I heard two words that scared me. Maggie said, "I'm pregnant."

At sixteen years old, still in high school, these were not the words I wanted to hear. I think I saw my life flash before my eyes, and it wasn't pretty. In fact, I recall it being filled with pictures of hard work, struggling to raise a baby with a girl I wasn't all that crazy about anymore. I had been raised with a sense of honor, and of responsibility. My mother had often warned me, with a phrase she used, that if I was going to stick it in I had better be prepared to take care of whatever came out.

The next four to six weeks were very strange. I kept seeing Maggie and was doing the best I could to prepare myself for becoming a father at the age of sixteen. During that time, however, I started noticing things that didn't seem right. Maggie had no problem telling my parents and sisters that she was pregnant, but she refused to say anything to her parents about it. I saw other things that made me realize she was a manipulative person. Then, one day Kay told me that Maggie had inadvertently let it out that she wasn't pregnant, that she was just saying that to keep me around because she didn't want me to break up with her. I was livid.

I took Maggie out that very night, and we went to one of the local hospitals. She asked what we were doing there, since I had not told her where we were going. I told her I wanted her to go inside and take a blood test and prove that she was pregnant. I told her if she didn't do it we were through. Of course she refused, and argued with me that I didn't trust her. I told her what Kay had told me. Over the course of the next hour we sat in the parking lot of the hospital arguing back and forth, because I refused to take her home unless she went in and took the blood test. Finally she broke down and admitted the truth. She was not pregnant.

I was lucky, I had spent over a month suspecting that I was going to be a father when I was far to young to be one. I learned that sex is not something teenagers should be involved in. Teenagers are not prepared for the consequences. Pregnancy is just one problem to deal with. There are a ton of diseases that a person can get from sex, and none of them are pleasant. After that experience, I did not have sex again until I was nineteen. I know condoms reduce the chances of pregnancy and transmittal of diseases, but they are not foolproof. Teenagers should not have sex. I don't care what the liberal crowd says about it, teenagers should abstain from sex until they are adults. After they become adults, if they are going to stick it in they should be responsible for whatever comes out.

Marriage doesn't change things

When I got together with Cindy, I thought I had learned a few things, since I had been divorced once already. Cindy asked me to marry her a few months after we started dating, and I said yes, but I insisted that it be at least a year-and-a-half away. I wanted to give her and I plenty of time to change our minds. I gave it time, but I never changed my mind even when I should have.

During the first year, we had some terrible roommates that added stress to our relationship, but they were just a part of the problem. Cindy couldn't hold down a job very well, and her income problems caused more than a few arguments between us. What money she did earn was spent on her, and I was the one paying for everything else. She also went out far too often, usually with her girlfriend Claire whom I couldn't stand. I was already twenty-five years old, and I had long outgrown the need to go out several times a week. She turned twenty-one right after we got together, so going out was a whole new experience for her, and it was one she enjoyed. Sometimes she went out four or five times a week. When she was at home, Cindy often spent hours on the phone, talking to her mom, talking to her dad, or talking to Claire. One night she spent over ninety minutes on the phone, then spent ten minutes with my daughter and I before announcing she was going to bed. I, of course, was furious.

We fought too much. That should have been the first clue. The second clue should have been how little Cindy seemed to want to be around. We were living together, but we were rarely together. Her work schedule didn't help, but her going out all the time really made it difficult for us to spend time with each other. There were other clues as well, like when Cindy was flirting with other guys on the internet, or when she was out with Claire and the two of them were flirting in the bars and nightclubs they went to.

We had a lot of problems, and I was dumb enough to think that things would change after we got married. . For one thing, I hoped that Cindy would mature, and that would cut down on how often she went out. I also hoped that she would learn to keep a job. During the four years that we were together, Cindy worked for ten different companies. She had a knack of leaving a job before she found another one, so there were often periods of weeks when she would have no income, and then she would fall behind on her bills and couldn't catch up.

Six months after we were married, Cindy left, saying that she wasn't sure she wanted to be married. I was devastated, and so was my daughter. I tried to talk to her, but she said she needed time to think and to figure out what she wanted. The weeks stretched into a month, and then two. I heard through the grapevine that Cindy and Claire were living together, going out all the time, and that she had no interest in coming back. Talking to her didn't help, and I got to a point when I decided to just leave her alone for a while. Time passed, and after about four months Cindy and I were talking again, and she told me everything I wanted to hear.

She said she was sorry for hurting my daughter and I. She said she'd made a mistake, she wanted us to be together, for the three of us to be a family, and she wanted to come home. Cindy said things would be different if I would give her another chance. I told her I would give her one chance, but that if she ever left again, for any reason, that it would be over between us, because I couldn't live like that. So, Cindy moved back in, and we had about four or five good months before she started going back to the way she was. Her self-centeredness reappeared, and it got worse. A little over two years after we were married, Cindy told me she was leaving again, and I told her I'd file for divorce because it was over.

Getting married doesn't solve problems in a relationship. People are who they are, and rarely do they change dramatically. Sometimes people will go through drastic events that will forever change them, but usually changes are subtle and take a long time to occur. I had the right idea in giving us time before tying the knot, but I should have followed through and ended the engagement before we married. Cindy and I were not compatible. She wanted someone to provide for her but she didn't want a relationship. She was selfish, and I was foolish to think she'd change. One of the most important lessons is to take relationships slow, get to know the other person before you make any kind of commitments.

When the person you are dating can't hold down a job, they will have a hard time helping you pay the utility bills after you're married. Your significant other who is more interested in hanging out with their friends will not build a lifelong relationship with you after you say your vows. A person who cannot commit before marriage will probably be unfaithful afterward. It is so important to find the right person and to make sure they are the right one. I have now been divorced twice, because the first one said she didn't want to be a mother, and the second was too wrapped up in herself and I didn't recognize it soon enough. Give your relationship time to grow before you ever consider marriage. You must learn what the person is like in so many ways. You have to see how they handle money, how they feel about children, what their views on religion are, and if they share your work ethic. Dave Ramsey, the financial guru of talk radio, often says that people need to agree on four key things: money, in-laws, children, and religion. If you don't agree on those things the relationship is probably doomed from the start. Divorce is a costly and messy process, and it would probably be avoided a lot more if people would spend more time really making sure they and their partner were compatible. I called this chapter Marriage Doesn't Change Things, but that is misleading. Marriage binds you legally to a person that maybe you shouldn't have been with in the first place. In a lot of states, marriage binds you to pay the other's bills, and entitles them to half of your property. These are the reasons why it is so important to discover who the person is before you marry, because marriage does change a few things. Marriage just doesn't change people.

Sex outside of marriage

When I married Mary, I told her that I would never cheat on her. I figured that was a pretty rotten thing to do to someone you loved, and I never wanted to have it happen to me. I told her that if she ever did cheat on our relationship, I would leave her immediately, because I could forgive a lot of things, but never that. A year and a half later, when Mary left, I was told by her uncle that she had been cheating on me, that she'd had a boyfriend for several months, and that everyone in her family knew it. I confronted her about it, and of course she denied it, but her uncle was a reliable guy and I figured it must have been true.

I was divorcing her anyway, because of many other reasons, but I knew I did not want to be with someone who had cheated on me. Because of what had happened, I told Cindy the same thing when we started dating. She said she would never cheat on me, because she agreed that it was a pretty low thing to do. As far as I know, Cindy never cheated on me while we were married, which is about the only good thing I have to say about her. As for myself, I wasn't so true.

Cindy had a couple of stepsisters, Alyssa and Angel. Both were a few years younger than Cindy was. Angel was finishing high school around the time that Cindy left, which was six months after we'd been married. Cindy told me she thought she'd made a mistake; that she didn't want to be married. Cindy had moved out and was living with her Dad. Whenever we talked, I got the feeling that she wasn't interested in coming back, or trying to make things better. Cindy had been gone about a month when Angel's graduation ceremony came up. I had told Angel that I would be at the ceremony for her, because graduating from high school is an important part of a person's life.

My daughter and I got to the ceremony late, and there weren't any seats left in the stands around the football field that they were using. A few people were already standing down toward one end of the field, so my daughter and I headed in that direction so we could at least sit in the grass. Also, there were other kids playing, which would keep my daughter entertained, since she was only four and was not likely to sit still for long. While the ceremony took place, my daughter played with one young girl who was about eight, and her mother started up a conversation with me. Her name was Lana, and her daughter was Abby. Lana was two years older than I was, and she was a single mother. During the two hours for the ceremony, we talked about different things while our kids played together, and at the end of the night we found ourselves lingering on the field still engaged in conversation while most everyone else cleared out. Finally, she said she had to go, because she was there to see her much younger brother graduate, and now had to go find him in the crowds of people that were left. Before she left, I asked for her phone number, saying that I had enjoyed talking with her and the kids had enjoyed playing together, and I wanted us to get together again. She agreed, and two weeks later we took the kids to the zoo. That was followed by a trip to McDonald's, and then she suggested we go miniature golfing. I had planned on going to my sister's for a barbecue that evening, but she said she wasn't ready for us to go just yet. I checked my watch, figured my daughter and I had some time, and we went golfing. During our eighteen holes, I had to borrow Lana's cell phone to call my sister and tell her I was going to be late, and in the process I got Lana and Abby invited over to my sisters with us.

What had started out as spending a couple hours together for the zoo and lunch turned into spending the rest of the day together. We'd gone from miniature golfing to Lana's house so she could change, and in the process we'd gone from driving separate vehicles to using just one. That meant that at the end of the evening when the barbecue was over, I had to drive Lana and Abby back home. When we got there, she invited us in, and after a little while the kids turned on a Disney movie to watch. Lana and I ended up in her bedroom, making out. Then we slept together.

Since I was still married to Cindy, I had cheated on her. I knew that we had been separated for over a month already, and it really looked like we were not getting back together, but I was still legally married to her, and I cheated on her. I also cheated myself, because I had never wanted to do such a thing. I suppose that it could be said that Lana was at fault. She told me later that she had decided she was going to sleep with me shortly after she'd met me. Looking back at things, it seems like she was trying to keep me around her that day, and since I had to drive her home in the evening she had a better chance of getting me in bed than if we'd had separate vehicles to drive. Still, I knew what I was doing, and I can't blame her for my decision to sleep with her. I had a choice, and I made it.

Lana and I slept together only twice, and after that we never did again. We spent the next couple of months hanging out with each other and letting the kids get to know each other, but we weren't intimate anymore. I don't know what her reasons were. From the beginning she had known about Cindy, and that might have had something to do with it, or she may have just decided she didn't want to be someone's rebound relationship. She would have been that if Cindy and I were over and Lana and I got together. As for my reasons, I felt pretty horrible about myself once I realized what I had done, and I didn't look at Lana quite the same way after that. I tried to be friends with her, but there was often something in my mind reminding me that I had broken a promise to myself and that she had been involved. After a few more months had passed, I started talking to Cindy again about us getting back together and soon Lana and I just quit being friends. We never had a disagreement or anything, just one day I quit calling her and she quit calling me. It was for the best anyway.

I had to tell Cindy about what had happened with Lana, and I did that even before we agreed to get back together. I needed her to know what had happened. She was understandably upset, but she agreed that she had been giving me signals that we were completely through and were not going to get back together, and she said she understood why I had given in. That still didn't make things any better as far as I was concerned.

Marriage is supposed to be a sacred thing. In the past, more people believed in the sanctity of marriage. Today, people get divorced or cheat on their spouse far too often. Marriage vows are not just idle words spoken once. They mean that you are committing yourself to just that one person, and you should consider that commitment to be for the rest of your life. Cheating on your marriage is a rotten thing to do, and there aren't any excuses for doing it. I can't make excuses, because I know what I did was wrong. I broke the trust that existed, and I have to live with that for the rest of my life. Now I am involved with Chrystel, and we are planning on getting married next year. I have been honest with her about what happened with Lana, and I hope she knows that I have learned a great lesson. I was faithful to Mary, and I was faithful to Cindy while we were together, even when things were miserable between Cindy and I. Chrystel and I have discussed our pasts and how infidelity can be so destructive to people. I know it is not what I want. I made my mistake in the past, and don't plan on repeating it, not for any woman. I don't want to hurt Chrystel, or myself, or let either of us down that way.

No matter what temptations you face, cheating on your marriage is wrong. It is destructive. It is not worth it in any way. Cheating on your spouse may cost you money, your career, your house, your kids, or your life. If you have any morals, you will not cheat. The decision is yours.

Know what you're getting into

After getting divorced for the second time, I spent four months avoiding women and trying to get things straightened back out for my daughter and I. I started talking to people in internet chat rooms at night for entertainment, because I couldn't go out. I'd put my daughter to bed at eight and I would spend the next two or three hours every night chatting. In April I met a woman named Gina. She lived in a small town about 80 miles away, had four kids, and was very interesting to talk to. One weekend about three weeks after I first started talking to Gina, my daughter and I drove down to meet them. She had three girls, Andrea, Dina, and Mindy, all from her first husband. She had a 23-month-old son, Joseph, from her second husband. My daughter's age was in-between Andrea's and Dina's, so she adored them and they her at first. My daughter and I went to the park and played on the playground equipment with them, and Gina and I talked for a while as the kids continued playing. Then we all went back to her place and watched a movie together before the evening was over and I had to drive back home. This first weekend visit was followed by a second, then a third, and the fourth weekend they came up to my house to spend the weekend. When we weren't together during the week, we kept in contact with each other nightly by means of the computer.

I started to think that Gina would be a great wife, because she was obviously family oriented and thought, therefore, that she couldn't be self-centered the way either of my ex-wives were. Things weren't as they seemed, though.

Gina very quickly indicated that she wanted us to be together. She made certain that I felt very happy whenever we were together, and she did a very good job of keeping her kids in line when my daughter and I were around. She would work hard to make home-cooked meals and she did everything possible to get me thinking about the two of us being together for the future. As I look back on the situation, I wonder how sincere Gina really was, because I often wonder if she was just after any man who would be willing to support her and her kids. She was living on government assistance at the time, and it was due to run out in nine months because of how long she'd been on it already. With having four kids, it made it very hard for her to work, and it also meant that very few men would be interested in her because of the number of kids she had.

I ended up proposing to Gina a few weeks after she started talking about us getting married. I thought that was what I wanted, because things seemed right. Gina had me convinced that we would be one great big happy family, and that she would never leave. That was one of the most important parts for me, since I had just gotten divorced for the second time in my life. We used some money I had to move her and the kids to live with us. That happened at the end of May, right after her kids got out of school. Having Gina move in changed a lot of things around the house. Not only did she come with four kids, she also had two German Shepherds, a 100 gallon fish tank, a bird, two cats, a fresh water turtle, and a cage full of rats. We managed to crowd most of her furniture into my three-bedroom house, although there wasn't a spare section of floor to be found anywhere.

This zoo was a headache waiting to happen, but I still didn't see it coming at that point. My daughter shared her room with Andrea, while Dina, Mindy and Joseph got the other room. What had once been a pretty quiet house, except for the occasional shouting matches with my ex-wife, had suddenly become a war zone. My daughter and I were used to things being a certain way. We had our routines that were suddenly altered by the presence of five other people and the menagerie of pets. My daughter had her own room for so long and now had to share. She'd had me pretty much all to herself and suddenly didn't. The kids were always fighting about something. The house was a disaster area every night. Putting the kids to bed took over an hour.

Gina didn't have much to do with the kids it seemed. I had been led to believe that she was very active in what they did during the day. Instead, Gina spent hours on the computer, visiting with her friends in chat rooms. The kids were left to play, destroying their bedrooms daily while she was occupied. She seemed to think that the way to make me happy was by having a home-cooked meal waiting on the table for me, so Gina would spend a couple hours in the kitchen making four and five course dinners to feed this army. While she did all this cooking, the kids continued their destruction to their bedrooms. When I got home, I got a good twenty-minute lecture on how my daughter had done one thing or another. Sometimes it was how she didn't want to share stuff. Other times it was how my daughter wouldn't listen to the kids and wouldn't do what they wanted to do. Never did I hear how Gina's kids acted during the day, as if I was lucky Gina was around because without her I wasn't raising my daughter right. I heard the way her kids acted many times myself. They ganged up on my daughter and outnumbered her three against one since Joseph wasn't old enough to act that way yet. They bullied her to the point that she would end up crying constantly, and she often got blamed for things that they did. If I stepped in and tried to tell Gina what the truth was, she would accuse me of favoritism, as if I wasn't supposed to look out for my daughter's well being.

Gina tried real hard to put herself and the kids firmly into the picture. She started calling my father 'Dad' the day she met him, and insisted that her kids call him 'Grandpa'. If I tried to do something with my daughter like we had done in the past, her kids immediately had to be included or else she got upset that I wasn't being fair. I got to the point where I could see the frustration and the hurt on my daughter's face, and it hurt me physically. I would have stomach pains daily. I couldn't sleep. My mind was always racing. When I would come home from work, Gina would be screaming at the kids to get the bedrooms cleaned up, and instead of being able to do something with them in the evening, I would have to sit back and watch all of them clean, then eat, then shower. We'd put them off to bed and I'd read them all a story. When I would hug my daughter goodnight, she'd squeeze me tight and occasionally whisper she missed me.

After one month, I realized what a mistake I had made. Toward the end of June, I asked Gina to move out. I told her I was sorry and I would help her in any way I could to get moved out and into any place she wanted. She wanted to go back to her town rather than stay in mine, so she could put the kids back into a school they were familiar with. The first thing she had to do was find a place to rent. That wasn't going to be so easy, though, since she had left without telling her landlord that she was moving. She also had not paid her remaining utility bills, figuring that she was going to be living with me and they wouldn't be able to get the money from her. Telling her and the kids was the hardest thing I have ever done. I told her one night, and the following morning told each of the kids individually. They didn't understand, but I couldn't explain to them. I couldn't handle the changes that had taken place, and it wasn't the right situation for my daughter and I. I didn't like the way Gina treated my daughter. So, I did everything I could to make things right again. I helped Gina find a house to rent in the same neighborhood they'd been in before. I rented a truck and helped her move down there. I paid to get the utilities on. I gave her some money to help her out since she was losing her government assistance in less than a year and would have to find work. Then, I came back home and tried to put my house back in order.

I had been completely wrong. I had moved too quickly to jump into a relationship without knowing anything about her and the kids. People talk about being on the rebound after a relationship ends, and I know exactly what they talk about. I was so hurt because my second wife had hurt us so much that I thought I would find someone who couldn't leave. Gina was on government assistance. Subconsciously I may have thought that I could rescue her and provide for her, and she would be so grateful that she would stay. I never really took the time to get to know her the way I should have. I didn't know that she ignored her kids because her priority was the chat rooms on the internet. I should have been really cautious about dating, and instead I had jumped into a situation that was totally wrong for me. I should have thought about what I was doing, and more importantly what effect it would have on my daughter. I didn't put any thought into it, though. I followed my heart and went with what felt right. That was a big mistake.

In any relationship, you have to get to know the person. You can only do this by spending time with them, and I don't mean spending time chatting on the internet. On the internet, you only get to see what the person wants you to see. You don't get to learn what they are truly like. If you don't have kids, you can take a few more risks than what a person with kids should take. You can date and possibly even live together without concerning yourself with how it affects a young developing child. Our culture has begun ignoring what is good for the children in favor of what feels good for the adults. We need to stop doing this, and take extra time to do what is right for all parties when there are kids involved.

I now believe that relationships need to be cultivated. You need to date, to talk, to share, and to experience new things in the company of the person you are with. You have to see how they respond to good things, and to bad experiences. It is your job to find out how they feel about money, work, life, kids, pets, religion, parents, and politics. The more you can agree with the other person, the stronger your relationship should be. Enjoy the journey of getting to know this other person, don't just rush things to set up house and play family. When you rush things you are asking for trouble. There will be something about the other person that you can't stand, and it will be magnified in so many ways that it will lead to a terrible relationship in one way or another. The best thing to do is give it time. Have the patience it takes to build a strong relationship, and you will improve your chances of having a successful one. Communication is the key to all of it. You will not find a person so much like you that you are a perfect couple like you see in the movies. There will be some strife, but you both will have to be willing to work at the relationship. A good relationship isn't a lot of work, but you do have to put the time in. You have to communicate your feelings, and you have to be able to admit when you are wrong. A wise person will know what they are getting into before they move in with someone, and they will know a great deal more before they will commit to marriage. Those wise people, however, who take the time to get to know each other and who understand what they are doing, will have the kind of marriages that last a lifetime.

They will have the kind of close, meaningful relationship that most will not. We must not be so swayed by our feelings that we do not listen to our minds. We must not be so driven by our physical desires that we do not heed logic. We must not be so blind that we don't know what we are getting into.

Smoking

I was fourteen years old when I started smoking. I was going to a Baptist church where the teenagers often hid behind one of the buildings to have a smoke. I guess I started for the reason that most kids do, because of peer pressure and the desire to fit in with my friends. At the time, there was a local convenience store where business wasn't so great, so the proprietor didn't care to whom he sold because cash was king. This was also back in the day when certain businesses, like the corner gas station, had cigarette vending machines. These are almost impossible to find today, but back then I could get cigarettes without a second thought. Adults finally realized that kids were purchasing from the machines because the machine couldn't check to see if the buyer was of the appropriate age or not. I think most of the machines disappeared around the time I was twenty, but I was buying them legally then, so I didn't care.

When I was sixteen, I had a job working during the summers for the state on a highway maintenance crew. It was good work, paid a little better than minimum wage, and was a lot more interesting than flipping burgers ever would have been. Since I was around adults all the time, I had a steady supply of cigarettes. One of the guys I worked with, Ray, smoked three packs of menthol cigarettes a day. I would often watch him light one up from the dying embers of the last one. He didn't mind sharing, so I got most of my cigarettes from him. The first year I worked with him, Ray was a small, wiry but muscular man in his mid fifties. The second year I worked for the highway crew, Ray got sick, and started losing weight, which he didn't have much of to spare. Ray had to quit his job, and very soon they found that he had lung cancer. He started on chemotherapy, and continued smoking. I was in the office one day about two months after Ray had been diagnosed, and he came in to talk to our supervisor. Ray looked shriveled, like he was over 90 years old. He'd lost all the hair on his head, and he coughed fiercely as he talked, a lit cigarette in his hand. I quit smoking that day. Ray died about two months later, the cancer had spread too far and the chemotherapy couldn't do anything for him. I stayed off the cigarettes for about a year after that, but I started again for one reason or another.

By the time I could buy cigarettes legally, I had quit and started back up again about six times. Sometimes I'd get disgusted with myself for doing it, realizing what a nasty habit it was, and I'd quit. It didn't matter though, because I always started back up again. If I quit buying because of how expensive cigarettes were getting, I would find a way to smoke by mooching off my dad or off my coworkers. It didn't matter to me that I was paying more for life insurance because I was a smoker, because I was young and dumb and didn't care. Sometimes, when I was dating a girl who didn't smoke, I would hide from her the fact that I did, so she didn't take it as a reason to dump me. Since I was never a heavy smoker, I could do this pretty easily. I always showered and changed before going out, so I would make certain the stench was not on my clothes or in my hair. If they did smell a trace amount on me, I could easily blame it on the second-hand smoke from being around my coworkers. It wasn't until later in life that I realized how pathetic my actions were.

When my daughter was born I was twenty-two, and had already been smoking off-and-on for eight years. I knew what the dangers were of smoking, but at the time didn't care about what I was doing to myself. I did care about my little girl though. There was a strict rule that there was no smoking in the vehicles, or in the house. That cut down on my smoking even more, and it made it easier to quit again. Still, the cycle of starting back up again continued. When my first wife left me, I started smoking again. In a way, that made me a bit more appealing to my second wife, because she smoked when we first got together. Then, I managed to quit again. When I went through the second divorce, I started smoking again, and I was still doing it over a year later when Chrystel and I got together. I was twenty-nine years old, and it had been fifteen years of playing around with cigarettes. Chrystel had struggled with smoking on occasion as well, and when we first got together she started smoking again because I was doing it. After two months, we sat down and talked about it, and decided that we didn't want to do it anymore. My daughter was seven years old at the time, and she knew from what they taught her at school that smoking was bad for a person. She wanted us to quit, and we had finally had enough ourselves. We realized that we were going to be a bad influence on her if we continued to smoke. So, we quit together, using each other for support. It is now a year-and-a-half later, and since the day we quit I have only broken down once, and I had one cigarette. Chrystel managed to quit with the same success.

Smoking is a terrible habit. It makes your clothes smell, and that smell lingers on your fingers and in your hair. It makes your breath stink and I can't imagine anyone enjoying kissing someone who smokes, because it is like sucking up an ashtray. The chemicals in cigarettes are addictive, and they are harmful to you. They won't get you right away, which is why most people, like myself, don't worry too much about it, but they will harm your body. You can ask almost anybody about what cigarettes can do to you. Start with the guy who has a whole cut in his throat to breathe because he got throat cancer. From there, talk to the guy on chemotherapy, where the cure can seem worse than the disease because of the treatments they subject you to. You can't ask my old buddy Ray, because the cancer took him over ten years ago, and I still find myself thinking about him from time to time. I wonder how much damage I have done to myself. I wonder if my body will be able to repair itself or not.

Smoking costs you, in one way or another. The money you put into cigarettes could be better spent elsewhere. Rather than burning up your money in the form of cigarettes, you could put it into clothes, stereos, your car, or anything else that is worthwhile to you. Smoking is expensive, and you will pay more for other things because of it. If you have a house, you'll pay more for insurance if you smoke, because you are more likely to cause a fire with a careless cigarette. If you get life insurance, you will pay more for it. You may pay more for medical insurance, and you will certainly pay more in medical costs throughout your life because smokers are often sicker and have more instances of cancer than non-smokers. Smoking just isn't worth the expense.

If you've never smoked, the advice I give is to not smoke. Talk to your doctor and to others, and learn what you could really be doing to yourself. Don't fall for peer pressure, because getting lung cancer isn't cool. If you're already smoking, I suggest you quit now. Get help if you need help quitting. Find the support you need to get you off the cigarettes and keep you off. That's all you have to do. You don't have to become an anti-smoking crusader at your school or your job. In the end, this is still a legal product for adults and adults who use it do so of their own free will. I made the mistake of smoking when I was young, but you don't have to.

Drinking

When I was between the ages of sixteen and eighteen I rarely drank alcohol, although a number of my friends did regularly at that age. I was too busy spending my free time driving around, enjoying the freedom of having a car and a license. After I turned eighteen, however, I started drinking at parties and when I was hanging out with a few choice friends. There was a clerk at the local convenience store who was convinced I was twenty-five so he never asked me for identification. I didn't have a fake license like some kids do, I just looked older and the way I carried myself apparently made me seem mature. I know the guy wasn't selling to just anyone, because on more than one occasion I saw him check the licenses of other people. Since the guy never asked me, I was the one who bought. Then, we'd go out in the middle of nowhere and we'd sit with the radio on in the car and we'd drink. Usually there were three of us, and sometimes there were five. I never bought more than a twelve-pack, so the guy at the convenience store never wondered who was helping me drink the beer. Even when there were five, there was still enough beer for each of us to enjoy sitting around drinking while the radio played.

Two of the guys I hung out with were under the age of eighteen. I worked with them at a restaurant washing dishes, and I knew them well enough to believe that they wouldn't turn me in for contributing to the delinquency of a minor. The problem was that they wanted to bring girls along with us all the time, and the girls were underage as well. I didn't know them quite as well, and after one particularly late evening when we were all out at one of our hidden spots, one of the girls got in trouble with her parents because they'd caught her sneaking back into her house. They could smell the beer on her breath, and they wanted to know where she'd been drinking. Fortunately for me, she didn't know my name, and there were enough of us working at the restaurant that her parents couldn't be certain whom she'd been out with.

I understood the trouble I could get into for underage drinking, and how much more trouble I would see if I was caught giving alcohol to other kids. I quit hanging out with that group, and stopped buying for other people. I was going to college then, and had too much to look forward to. I didn't want to screw everything up by drinking when I was underage. I know I never got caught, and I realize I was lucky. Not all kids are so lucky. I know several of my friends got busted for underage drinking after I quit hanging out with them. I know some of them had to pay pretty stiff fines, and most if not all of them had to do some type of community service.

There are so many other reasons not to drink when you're young. One of the guys I worked with liked to take girls out and get them drunk. He knew that the more inebriated a girl got, the more likely he was to get her into bed. That is rape. The girls were not capable of making the right decisions, and he knew it. No one can tell me that drinking is worth getting a sexually transmitted disease or having an unwanted pregnancy occur. I can't imagine hearing a girl say she didn't care she got raped, as long as she got drunk. Drinking is not worth it. Alcohol is a drug, and it should be respected. It is meant for adults, and it should not be abused, and most kids don't realize that. There are still a lot of adults that don't realize it.

In the town I live in, three kids in their late teens just died because of a vehicle accident where alcohol was involved. If fines and doing community service aren't bad enough, tell me how the risk of dying is worth drinking. You don't even have to get into a car for alcohol to kill you, there are kids each year who die from drinking too much alcohol in a short time, and their body can't handle it.

It has taken me a few years, but I have learned what my limit is. I am an adult, so I am allowed to drink, but that doesn't make it right for kids. If you are under twenty-one, don't drink. It's not worth the headaches, the vomiting, or the stomach cramps. I'll say it again, just so you remember. If you are under twenty-one, don't drink. When you are legal, don't abuse it. It's okay to drink a few at a party, but you better sober up before you drive. If you're absolutely going to get drunk, stay home, and don't go anywhere. When you're drunk you don't think clearly, and your reactions are slower. If you're throwing a party, and you are serving alcohol, you are responsible for your guests. If you let them drink and get behind the wheel, you will be held liable for your part. It's not worth it. Be responsible, because the consequences of mistreating alcohol can be disastrous.

Drugs

I had an ear infection when I was younger, probably around the age of nine or ten. I didn't realize that I had one, though, and it got pretty bad and was affecting my hearing. My parents would catch me sitting a few feet from the television with the volume turned way up to deafening levels, just so I could hear. They would have to raise their voices for me to understand what they were saying. After a few days of this, they took me to see a doctor, who diagnosed the problem and gave me some form of antibiotic.

They let me administer the pills to myself, which was okay because I was pretty good at telling time and knew how often I was supposed to take the medicine. The problem was that I missed one dose, and being as young as I was, I decided to double up the next time to make up for it. The effects of that left a lasting impression on me. I remember feeling strange, like my brain was not connected to my body, and things seemed to be spinning which shouldn't have been. I didn't like the feeling at all. Probably some of the effects were exaggerated, but I learned from that experience that I did not want to have anything to do with things that left me feeling that out of control.

I grew up from then on knowing that I didn't want to do drugs. That didn't keep me from being friends with people who did, however. In tenth grade, I was close friends with a girl named Margaret, who smoked marijuana regularly. I'd go to her house on occasion, and Margaret and a few other people would light up a joint and pass it around the room, but it was always understood that I wasn't participating. I'd sit by the window with the fan blowing air into the room, or I'd go outside and wait until they were done. In twelfth grade, I hung out at parties where half the people there were smoking a joint. I'd sit with them but the only thing I smoked was a cigarette. They would offer a hit to me, and I'd turn them down, and everyone was okay with that.

I knew only a couple of people who ever did anything more than marijuana. Cocaine was pretty rare, but a few friends were into popping whatever prescription drugs they could get their hands on, and they raided medicine cabinets at their friend's homes to get their fix. Sometimes my friends didn't like it when I told them that drugs were stupid, but most of them didn't care one way or another how I felt about them. What mattered to them was the drugs, and what mattered to me was being clean.

When I was a little older, I prided myself on knowing that if I was applying for a job, I would always pass the drug screen tests. I never had to worry about random testing. A lot of the jobs I had held would fire you if you couldn't pass the test. Keeping a job is just one of the many reasons not to do drugs. I have seen how much damage drugs can do. We had close family friends who had two daughters, Denise and Antonia. My sisters spent so much time with Denise and Antonia that they were like cousins to us. Antonia was my age, and Denise a couple of years older. Both were very bright and were good looking in their teens. Denise probably experimented with a few drugs in her youth, but that was all. She went on to have a career in the military, and in her early thirties is still very bright and is still good looking. Antonia was the one that abused drugs, and still does to this day. She is jobless, doped up so much all the time that her kids suffer from lack of good attention, and she has lost her good looks. I see her on occasion because her kids go to the same school that my daughter does. Antonia looks haggard, run down, and her expressions are often vacant. I do not have to wonder how much effect the drugs have had, because her appearance shows that they have affected her considerably.

You can't tell me that drugs are harmless. I know people who couldn't get the job they wanted because they wouldn't clean up their act. I know people who are doing time in jail because they got involved in drugs and got caught with them. Drugs cost a lot of money, and they will get you into a lot of trouble if you are caught with them. Even if you are never in any legal trouble because of drugs, they will still cause you trouble. Drugs affect your brain, and your body. They can shorten your life or take it altogether.

I made the decision for myself that I was never going to do drugs. I wanted to be able to tell my children honestly that I never did drugs. Of all the bad decisions I made over the years, I made the right decision regarding drugs. I never experimented, and I am very proud of that fact. Drugs should be avoided. You can make the decision for yourself whether you hang out with people who do them or you avoid those people, but make the decision to avoid drugs. It will be one of the most rewarding decisions of your life.

Have enough insurance

Early one morning several years ago, I was taking my daughter to the sitter before I had to get to work. I had neglected putting gas in my little Chevy S-10 the night before, and it was on fumes. The gas gauge had never worked in the time I owned the truck, so I attempted to keep track of my gas based on the number of miles I drove. I had already neglected to put gas in the truck for two days, so I figured today had to be the day to get gas, before I ran out. Unfortunately, I had misjudged somewhere, because the engine died from lack of fuel soon after leaving the house.

Where I live, about seven miles west of the city, we are at a slightly higher elevation, so I have a gentle decent along the state highway to get into town. Since I was out of gas but was still rolling, I figured I was going to try to coast as far as I could get. My daughter was four years old then, and was not old enough for a long walk to get gas, and I did not have a cell phone to call anyone.

I put my hazard lights on, and moved into the far right-hand lane. Coasting, I was doing about 35 miles-per-hour where the speed limit was posted at 55 and the traffic normally did closer to 70. The sky was clear and the road has great visibility, and it was still early enough that there was little traffic. I kept checking my rear-view mirror though, because I knew I had little maneuverability since the engine was off with no gasoline to power it.

As we coasted, I saw a car come up behind us in the same lane I was in. There was no other traffic on the road around either of us. I watched the car and realized it was not moving into the other lane to pass me, so I started to steer off the road, hoping the driver was going to see us and go around. At almost the last second, the driver must have looked, because I watched in the mirror as the rear tires locked up and I could hear the squeal of the brakes and the screech of the tires. The front of the car swerved to the left, and I knew if they kept going in that direction they would miss us. Apparently the driver had lost complete control, however, and the front of the car came back around. They struck us from behind, spun us both and pushed us off the road into the ditch.

My daughter was strapped in tight in her car seat, and was not injured. I think the only thing that affected her about the accident is she now is distraught about the possibility of running out of gas. I struck my head on the side window of the truck as we were spun, and I had quite a headache. The cops came as did the paramedics and an ambulance. The passenger in the other car was an elderly woman, and she was complaining of severe chest pains, so the ambulance took her away. The driver of the car admitted to the cops that she was speeding, and she was also talking with her passenger so much that she was not paying attention to the road. She was cited. The vehicles were towed away, and I got a coworker to come out and get my daughter and I.

I had medical insurance through work, so I got checked out and they said I didn't have a concussion, just some bruising and a headache. They checked me out for whiplash, and pronounced me okay. My daughter was fine as well, which was a major relief. Since I was not at fault, I notified my insurance company of the accident but did not file the claim with them. I filed the damage claim with the other driver's insurance company, and at first they were helpful. They put me into a rental car and sent the truck to the Chevrolet dealer to get an estimate of the damages. When they got the estimate, they determined that my truck wasn't worth fixing, and they called me with a settlement offer.

At the time, the truck was eight years old and I owed $4,000 on it. I had bought it used, and had only had it for two years. The insurance company offered me $2,000 for the truck. They said it was the best offer they could give me considering the trucks age, mileage, and condition. The truck was in great shape, didn't have any rust, and mechanically was perfect prior to the accident, but they wouldn't budge on the offer at first. Someone at work suggested I let them know about any major mechanical repairs done recently, and I notified them of a clutch replacement six months before the accident that had cost me $600. For that, they allotted me an additional $200. Then, the agent said he would offer me $400 for pain and suffering I had experienced in the accident, which brought the total I would receive up to $2,600. They were still offering me $1,400 less than what I owed on the loan, and still I would have nothing left for a down payment on another vehicle.

I checked the Kelley Blue Book and found that they valued the truck at pretty much what the insurance company was offering, so that was no help. I told the insurance agent that I was considering contacting the state insurance commission, and he said he was operating within state law. He suggested that I file a claim with my own insurance company, let them pay the claim, and his company would reimburse them. I didn't like that idea because I would have had to pay the deductible on the claim, and the accident had not been my fault. I searched for a way to make the other driver's insurance company take responsibility. Then, I found a truck very similar to mine that was being offered for sale at $4,200. I immediately called the insurance agent, and told him that vehicles similar to mine were selling for much more than he was offering me. He told me that if I could send him classified private-party advertisements of three vehicles similar to my truck, then he would pay the higher amount. I found four. I faxed him the proof, and I waited. I contacted him daily for three days, trying to find out if he was ready to settle the claim, and I got the run-around from him. Finally, I threatened to call a lawyer, and I told the insurance agent that not only would I get the settlement he'd agreed to pay but his company would have to pay my lawyers fees as well. Finally, he sent the paperwork and the settlement check, for $4,200 for my truck and $500 for pain and suffering. I paid the bank off for the loan, and had the rest for a down payment on another vehicle.

I learned that insurance companies are not overly friendly to work with. I also learned that they don't want to do what is right for the consumer, because their settlement agents are trained to try to get you to settle for the very least amount. I was fortunate that I didn't have to settle for the lower amount and pay the difference myself, but that does happen to a great number of people today. Vehicles depreciate in value so quickly that if you got a brand new vehicle and had it destroyed in an accident a month after it came off the lot, you'd be offered about 75% of what you owe on it. One of my ex-wives bought a car and had an accident six months after she got it. Her insurance was not enough to cover what she owed, so she spent the next two years paying the remainder of a loan for a car that was totaled. One of my sisters has been forced to do the same thing, as a car she bought last year for $15,000 was wrecked recently and they only paid her $9,000 for it, leaving her to pay off the balance.

Insurance is a big expense, but it is necessary. For automobiles, you should carry full coverage insurance unless the vehicle is worth less than $2,000. You should carry safety-glass coverage, because a broken windshield is expensive to replace and some of the other side windows and rear windows are even more expensive. Above all, if you owe money on the vehicle, you should probably have gap coverage. This is an additional insurance where you pay a little more each month, but if you lose a vehicle in an accident and have the gap insurance, they will pay off what you owe, not just what the vehicle was valued at. This is very important if you don't want to spend two or three years paying off a vehicle you can no longer drive.

Medical insurance is something else everyone should have. I have heard too many times that people can't afford medical insurance for their family, and then something happens and they have tens of thousands of dollars of medical bills. Usually these people end up filing bankruptcy. Unfortunately, the people who claim medical insurance is too expensive are often the same people who have their priorities all wrong and who would rather have a nice new car or something else they can't afford instead of making sure they have insurance. I know having a new shiny car is a status symbol and having medical insurance isn't, but I would rather sacrifice and drive an older vehicle so that my family is insured. You may want to consider living in a smaller house, driving a slightly older but less expensive vehicle, or doing without cable television or dining out or whatever else you can so that you can afford to have the medical insurance you need. Chances are that there will come a time in your life when you need it, and it will be very costly financially and emotionally if you do not have it.

There are many other types of insurance, such as life, fire, homeowners, renters, and disability. They are expensive, but it is more costly to your wallet if you don't have it and need it. Check into each of these, talk to several insurance agents, and get the advice of people you trust to help you make the right decisions about what insurance you need. Compare not just the cost but the coverage you get before you make a decision. Then, periodically review your insurance to make sure it still covers what you need it to. If you have added to your home, to your vehicles, to your family or whatever, make sure you have it covered so you are not surprised to find that you were underinsured. Be cautious as always, though, because not all insurance is necessary. Some products are better than others, and some companies are better to deal with, but it all comes down to a bit of a gamble, because you're gambling you'll need the insurance, and they're gambling you won't.

Go to college

I started college right after high school. I had an aptitude for computers, and my supervisor at work and several other people encouraged me to go to college and do something with computers. The first year I went I had a scholarship from the local electric company, which paid for all my classes and my books. I was working full time plus taking a full schedule of classes at college, and I was extremely busy with homework. Still, it was a great experience.

My favorite classes were my accounting classes. I had a remarkable teacher, Mr. Braatz, who taught that it was important that you find the work you enjoy, and then excel in that, rather than trying to do something just because of the money or the prestige or because it is expected of you. My writing class the first year was enjoyable, but I had some difficulty during the second semester because that writing teacher wanted us to constantly analyze other people's work. I often would work my papers over three times before turning them in, and I still would not find the concept he thought the author was commenting on. Even with the difficulty of satisfying the teacher, I still did well enough in that class.

My philosophy class was very intriguing, and it opened my mind to thinking about things in ways I had never considered before. I found that college was much more enjoyable than high school, because the people really wanted to be there, and since most were paying their own way, they weren't there to goof around. Considering the way kids acted in high school toward their teachers, it was remarkable to see how much better college classes were.

I ended up cutting back on the number of classes I enrolled in the following year, because working a full time job and taking that many classes was just too much. Then, when my daughter was born, I found it necessary to skip a semester or two here and there, but I found the means to go the rest of the time. When I went through my divorce, my sister and my dad were there to help me out by watching my daughter while I attended class. I kept going, because I did not want to give up on my dream of getting a college degree. I was the first one in my immediate family to go to college, and I was determined to succeed.

Along the way, I learned many things about myself. I found that even with the talent I had with computers, I did not wish to be a computer programmer, although that was what I had chosen for a course of study. I loved interacting with people, and had a greater aptitude for business than strictly for computers. After a time, I found that I wanted to be in business management instead, but by then I was already three-quarters of the way through the number of courses I needed to complete my associate's degree as a computer programmer / analyst. I decided to continue with my studies in computers, and get the degree, and use it as a basis for a career in business.

This past May, twelve years after I graduated from high school, I graduated from college with high honors. My diploma hangs on my dining room wall, and a copy of it has a space on the wall above my desk at work. I found over the years that Mr. Braatz was correct. It is rewarding to find work you enjoy, and then to do your best and excel at it, rather than focus on the money that is made. No amount of money will make up for a career you do not enjoy. No job title will make up for having to work in conditions you abhor. It is much more sensible to find something you are good at, and to do it well. Generally, when you enjoy your job it becomes a career, and you do well in it and succeed.

Going to college opened doors for me that would have been closed if I only had a high school diploma. I learned more about myself and the world around me than I would have otherwise. I met interesting people, and learned from them things that I could apply in my own career and in my own life. There are so many options out there that everyone should strongly consider going to college. There are scholarships, or you can pay for it as you can afford it. You may have the option of having your parents assist you, or you could consider joining the military to get the benefits of having your schooling paid for because of your service to the country. The last thing I would ever consider is taking out student loans, because too many people end up deeply in debt because of them, but people will use this option as well. However it is paid for, you should figure out how to go to school. The rewards are endless, and even if you find your life leads you down a path different from the one you started on, as I did, you will benefit from the experience of going to college. You will always benefit from learning.

The best time to have kids

When I was twenty-one years old, I started dating Mary. She was only seventeen at the time. We found out that she was pregnant after we'd started talking about getting married, but we weren't ready. I wasn't quite ready to have a kid, but I was going to be a father and there was nothing changing that.

There was a lot to deal with in having a baby, and I wasn't prepared. Most people aren't prepared regardless of their age and I was still pretty much a kid myself. I suddenly had to come up with the money for all kinds of things that we needed. Fortunately for me, a guy I worked with, Kevin, and his wife, Karen, had decided they were ready to get rid of their baby furniture and get new things for their son, so I got a few things from them for a really good price. I had the crib and the changing table, and a car seat. My sisters had both had girls three years before, and they had kept most of the clothes to pass down, so there were plenty of outfits if we had a girl. Even with these things to help us out, it was still a struggle to pay for things. The added medical insurance was a real killer. We had options of government assistance, but I refused because I had been brought up to pay my own way, and I didn't want to ask for help. As it turned out, though, Mary was anemic, so the government helped us out with a little bit, by providing milk and eggs and a few essentials to make sure Mary and our daughter got the nutrition they needed.

Having a baby changes a person, and perhaps more so when you have one at a young age. You no longer have the freedoms you once had. You have to be prepared to give up a lot, because of the child you have to provide for. I remember what it was like when my friends could go out after work without having to think about it. When you have a kid, you have to take care of them or you have to find someone else to watch the baby so you can have a break. You can't just leave the kid at home alone so you can go do what you want. Unfortunately, too many young people who have kids during their teenage years think that they can just leave the kid with someone else while they get on with their life. Even people in their early twenties sometimes have problems with accepting responsibility for the life they created.

When you have a kid, you have to be there for them. It is your responsibility to provide for them, to feed them, teach them, protect them, and love them. Many young people are too self-absorbed to be able to do this, though. Mary and I divorced partially because she did not want to be a mother anymore. She was barely twenty at the time. I suspect that a lot of the divorces that occur in this country are because young people become parents too soon, and they crack under the pressure after a time. Other people think only for themselves, and not for the child they created. I know of a mother who left her kid with her parents because she was in the military and wouldn't give up her career. Ramona was stationed in Arizona when I met her, while her child was being raised over two thousand miles away by his grandparents. This is hardly responsible parenting in my book.

I was twenty-two when my daughter came into this world, and she is eight now. I have learned a lot over those eight years. I have made many mistakes, and I paid the price for them and she paid the price with me on some of them. What I have learned regarding children is that for most people, it would be better to wait until they are over twenty-five or twenty-six before they have kids. Actually, I suspect most people shouldn't even consider marriage until then. There is so much to experience when you get out of high school, that you should not be considering starting a family.

There are people who miss out on the opportunity to go to college because they have the responsibility of raising a child. There are those who wanted a career in the military and couldn't do it because they had a family. From the age of eighteen to twenty-five is the time to make mistakes that don't necessarily hurt other people. It is the time to occasionally stay out all night partying and being dumb, of being late to work and maybe getting in trouble because of it. If you get fired, no one suffers but yourself. These are the years for learning and for living on your own. This is the time of your life to figure out what you enjoy doing, so that maybe you can build a career on it.

When you have lived on your own for a few years and have figured out a few things about the world then you will be better prepared for a serious relationship. You may not have finished your education, but at least by the age of twenty-five you should have gotten through most of it. By then you may have had a few jobs, and might have even worked hard enough to put yourself in a position where you're making decent wages. Most importantly, you will have had years of living for yourself where you could be self-centered, and by age twenty-five you should be at the stage where you are maturing and are more capable of handling other responsibilities. Imagine a world where people put off getting married right out of high school and having kids. You could be one of those people who put things in the right order, by delaying the family until the right time. You could get your life somewhat in order before you get involved with another person, and chances are you will have a better and longer lasting relationship then. You would be better prepared, both financially and mentally, for raising a child when you were older. This is a decision you will have to make early on, because then you will take the steps needed to delay starting a family. There is no reason why you can't delay getting married and having kids. Even if you are in a great relationship in your early twenties, you can make the decision to wait. If the relationship is that good and it lasts, then it will be that much stronger when you're a few years older and are ready to get married. If the relationship turned out to not be so good, you may have saved yourself the headache and heartache of divorce and child-custody disputes. You do not have to be in such a rush to create a family. Go, live your life, and when you're older, then find that special someone that you want for the rest of your life. Marry them when you're a few years older, more mature, and are ready for the responsibilities. Then, have fun raising your kids together, the way things were meant to be.

Money and credit (part 1)

My first wife, Mary, and I were living at my dad's house when our daughter was born. We needed a place of our own, and I was looking for anything that I could afford in a half-way decent neighborhood. My daughter was born in February, and by the end of March I had located an older single-wide two bedroom trailer in a mobile home park. The price wasn't bad, and the monthly lot rent was reasonable. We moved in just after April began.

I had recently purchased a car, and still had to pay off the loan on the Jeep that Dan had conned me out of, and now I had a monthly payment on the trailer and for the space rent for the trailer. Mary was not working, since she was to stay at home and take care of the baby, so everything came out of one income. I was twenty-two years old, and was responsible for earning the money needed to provide everything for my family. I had it all, medical insurance, car payment, car insurance, house payment, lot rent, payment on the Jeep loan, and I had credit cards.

I started with one credit card, with only a $100 credit limit. I would use it each month and would pay at least half of it off each month, sometimes paying all of it. Then I got a second card, with a $1,000 credit limit and with a low introductory interest rate. I transferred the balance from the $100 card to the new card and canceled the first card. When the interest rate went up on the second card I got a third and transferred the balance again, but this time I kept both cards. They were a necessity, I thought. Mary and I used them to buy groceries whenever I didn't have the money in my checking account. Christmas presents and birthday presents went on the credit cards. We couldn't afford half of what we bought, but I rationalized that I could afford the monthly payments, so we bought stuff anyway.

Banks do a good job of selling debt. We soon had three credit cards, and had balances on each of them. It got to a point where we would borrow from one credit card just to pay another. I was transferring balances back and forth constantly, because by transferring I got an extension on when the monthly payment was due. We didn't realize what a hole we were digging for ourselves.

We got bailed out of that mess only because Mary received an insurance settlement for a vehicle accident she'd been in. We paid off the credit cards and the rest of what we owed and started over. Unfortunately, the debt cycle started over again too.

Money and credit (part 2)

Mary and I got a divorce. I spent $1,800 on a lawyer and I got custody of my daughter, and life went on. The Toyota I was driving was falling apart, so I traded it in for a six-year-old Chevrolet S-10. The S-10 came with payments, of course, but they were nothing I couldn't handle. I had a house payment, a truck payment, insurance on the truck, medical insurance, house insurance, life insurance, flood insurance, groceries, utilities and daycare. Then I started using the credit cards again. By the time Cindy moved in I owed the credit cards about $1,700.

Cindy and I had a screwed up relationship right from the start. The money she earned was hers and she contributed almost nothing to the household income. If something around the house broke, I paid to fix it. I paid the utilities, I paid for the groceries, and I paid for everything else. I even used my credit cards to help her keep her car repaired. We got married a year-and-a-half after we got together and financed most of that on the credit cards. We bought Cindy a new car with an equity loan on the house. She made these payments since it was her car, and I paid the rest. The credit cards kept being used. When Cindy and I got a divorce, just over two years after we'd been married, we were over $15,000.00 in debt on the credit cards, and had a first and second mortgage on the house. We were typical American consumers, spending money like there was no tomorrow.

When Cindy left, she said she couldn't afford the car. I was forced to sell it at a loss, since cars are a lousy investment. They depreciate much faster than you could ever believe. Since I was left with the equity loan on my house and Cindy refused to pay for any of the bills she helped create, I was forced to file bankruptcy on the credit cards so that I could keep my house. My credit was shot, but I managed to hang onto the house so my daughter and I still had a place to live.

Nowadays I am driving around in a twenty-year-old pickup. It's one of those that should have a "Don't Laugh, It's Paid For" bumper sticker on it. I try to save money so I can pay cash for everything. The only credit cards I carry are for gasoline, and I pay those balances in full every month. I do without things I can't afford, and I sleep a little better at night because I am not worrying about being behind on the bills. Money is still tight each month, but things are getting better. I have a little emergency fund set aside to take care of the unexpected things that I used to reach for the credit card for.

I learned most of my new ideas regarding money from a guy on the radio named Dave Ramsey. He hosts a radio talk show where he advocates people working feverishly to get out of debt, and thereafter maintaining their life by saving up and paying cash for the things they want, rather than financing them and helping the banks get rich. Dave doesn't like people filing bankruptcy, so in my situation he'd have probably said I should have sold off my house, paid off the credit cards, and gotten a place to live that I could afford. I found Dave on the radio almost a year after I'd filed bankruptcy, though, so I did things differently than he would suggest, but he does have a lot of great ideas about money management that I do follow.

There are far too many people filing bankruptcy nowadays, and I was one of them. There are too many couples arguing about money. I don't want to do that anymore. I am willing to do without if I can't afford something. I am not going to saddle myself with debt all over again. Being broke sucks, but being broke and having the bill collector calling you at work is even worse. I know, I have been there.

There is nothing wrong with living modestly. I have known a lot of people who have a lot of stuff, and they are driving around in vehicles that cost $35,000 off the lot. Just because they look like they have money doesn't mean they do. What these people have is debt, and a lot of it. I don't want to have to take a second job to pay for my stuff. I would much rather have the time to spend with my daughter and the new woman in my life. We have rediscovered the joy of entertaining ourselves, of being a part of each others lives. We play board games, and we read aloud to each other from a book rather than watching cable television in silence. We don't live totally frugal lives, as one might think I am suggesting, because we still go out occasionally and we still eat out pretty often. We took two mini vacations this year. What we have learned is that we try to pay cash for everything. If we can't pay cash for it, we can't afford it and don't need it. People need to learn again how to distinguish their needs from their wants. Everyone needs to learn how to budget their money, so they can have the money they want for what is important to them, rather than buying on credit and paying interest. Debt is not a good thing. I understand without taking on some debt, most people could never acquire a home for themselves, but beyond a first mortgage on your house I think debt should be avoided at all costs.

I stop and think occasionally about how much stuff really cost me before I learned my lesson about managing money and credit. When I factor in the interest fees, the occasional over limit charges, and the late fees, things were pretty expensive. I understand why the banks have all the money, because of how much interest people pay because they cannot curb their wants. I was tired of living like this, but I knew I brought it on myself. It was up to me to make the changes, and I have and so far I have succeeded. Still, learning these lessons for myself is not enough. Already, I plan on teaching my daughter how to live on less than what she makes. I will try to instill in her the desire to remain debt free, and I will try to teach her how to be happy with what she's got. I will teach her to save and how to budget. If I can help her learn this valuable lesson, perhaps hers will be the marriage where they don't fight over money. Maybe she will never lose sleep worrying about paying the credit card bills. Perhaps I can save her from the troubles I have been through.

Relationships

I had been through much and had made a lot of stupid mistakes concerning women by the time I was twenty-nine. I had been married at twenty-one, divorced just after turning twenty-four, married again a month before I turned twenty-six, and divorced again at age twenty-eight. I'd followed my second divorce with getting very involved with a woman I knew next to nothing about. She came with four kids and a menagerie of pets. I discovered quickly that that relationship wasn't going to work, and I got out of it the best way I knew how before too much time went on.

I knew I didn't want to be alone for the rest of my life, but I also wanted to find the right woman, so I started dating again after a few months. I found women who were ready to jump into a relationship and I wasn't ready, and I found women who were so cautious about starting a new relationship that they seemed to only want to date via telephone. After a while, I had a few unremarkable dates with different women I didn't have anything in common with, and then I met Julie. We got along great together and had an easy rapport with each other. The holidays approached and I had someone to hang out with, although we had mutually agreed that we were not going to date each other. Instead, we became friends and enjoyed each others company. I had her to my company's Christmas dinner party, and she invited me to parties at her friends houses. She met us at school one night for a talent show my daughter was involved in. We went out for New Years and rang in the new year together. Life wasn't so bad, because I had a friend to talk to and go out with, but I wasn't in a relationship, either. Hanging out with Julie had allowed me to stop searching for a relationship, and that is usually when one will find you.

I came home eight days into the year 2002 to find a note taped to my front door. It was addressed to my ex-wife, Cindy, and I, and it read, "I hope you guys still live here. Let's see – It's Chrystel – Raymond's friend, William' ex-girlfriend. You know, the one who moved to New Jerky land. I'm back!" The note ended with a phone number and "I've missed you guys!" I remembered Chrystel, and had often wondered how she'd been doing since she'd moved to New Jersey with her parents. It had been four-and-a-half years since I had seen Chrystel. Cindy and I had only been engaged then, and Chrystel was supposed to have been one of Cindy's bridesmaids, but she'd backed out and had not come back to attend the wedding. Since the note was addressed as it was, apparently she had not heard that Cindy and I had been divorced. I called the number, and got an answering machine. I left a message for her, saying that I had a few things to catch her up on, and she should call me back. I heard from her within an hour, and she said she'd come visit later that evening.

Chrystel's visit turned into a late night session of reminiscing and tale-telling. She told me that she'd actually been back in town for three months, and I admonished her for taking so long to look us up. Chrystel and I had known each other really well before she'd moved, because she'd always been hanging out at my house, and it didn't take us long to see that we were interested in each other. I admitted that I'd been attracted to her in the past, but she'd been with William and I'd said nothing then. By the time she'd broken up with him, I'd already been engaged to Cindy, so she had said nothing either about feelings she'd had for me. We both agreed that it was probably for the best that we hadn't known in the past of our feelings for one another, because at the time Chrystel had still had some maturing to do. She'd done that in the intervening years in New Jersey.

My daughter asked Chrystel to move in, and I told her I felt the same way. Two weeks went by, and Chrystel and I had been together everyday during that time, so she moved in because she was there all the time anyway. We had already talked about the future, and about being together. I know the timetable was dreadfully short, but I had known Chrystel in the past and felt the risk was greatly reduced. Chrystel and I had been close friends in the past, and we were able to build on this to form a strong foundation for our relationship. We use everything we have at our disposal to keep the relationship healthy and alive.

Neither of us expects the relationship to be perfect. We have our ups and downs, although with Chrystel I have experienced a lot fewer downs than I ever did with Mary or Cindy. We occasionally have our bad days, but it is pretty rare that we ever lose our tempers with each other. Instead, our biggest challenge has been forging a family when my daughter has been guarded about getting close to Chrystel for fear that she may someday leave as well. We try to keep our communication open and honest with each other, so we can handle the problems that come along.

There are problems in every relationship. Dave Ramsey, the financial guru of talk radio, often tells his listeners that people need to agree on four key things in order to have a healthy marriage. These four things are: in-laws, children, money and religion. There are other things as well, but these four things are pretty important. Even though Chrystel and I are not married yet, we understand that these things are important in a relationship as well as in a marriage. Chrystel and I have argued about in-laws on both sides, but after a year-and-a-half together we have come to some understandings about the subject. We are in agreement about religion, but sometimes the subject of politics gets to us because we have different views there. We might not always agree on how to raise children, but we both share the view that the family is important. We spend lots of time with my daughter, playing games and reading to her, so that she sees that family is important and she knows that she is loved. We have been doing our best to help my daughter understand that Chrystel is making a commitment to stay, to be a part of her life, and that she is not going to disappear from my daughter's life like others have done. We know there will be issues in the future because Chrystel will be a step-mother, and there is usually conflict when children get older, but we are prepared to face it together because we know it is what we both want.

We have had some issues concerning money, because I make more than Chrystel does, but we have begun working that problem out as well. I had learned to budget my money over a year ago, and it allowed me to save and set aside an emergency fund, which I considered really critical because I had to file bankruptcy in the past and had no credit cards to rely on if something unexpected happened. Chrystel has been more of a free-spirit with her money, and had nothing set aside when she suddenly needed emergency dental work done. Since I had money I was able to help her, although she resented it and our money issues became more noticeable in our occasional arguments. Now, Chrystel and I have talked about the issue and she is trying to budget her money the way I do, and already she is starting to see the benefit to it. Also she has been working her fingers to the bone and recently got a raise at work plus a lot of overtime, so the difference in our incomes has been less and we have not had nearly as many problems as a result.

The reasons we are doing so well together are many, but I think I can identify a few of them. Chrystel and I respect each other. She respects my thoughts and how I have raised my daughter and provided for her. I respect her willingness to get involved in raising someone else's child, her achievements in her work over the years and most recently as she builds her career. I respect her willingness to volunteer, whether for the volunteer fire department or helping out in my daughter's classroom. Chrystel and I also communicate with each other, which is a key part of our relationship. We still say things occasionally that the other interprets wrong, but we talk and come to an understanding and that makes all the difference in the world at times. We share the chores around the house, whether it is laundry or dishes, vacuuming or dusting. We make time for each other but also give each other some space to pursue our own hobbies. We have come to an understanding that we will not have a utopian relationship, but we will have a good one. We have made a commitment to each other that this is for life, so we do our best to make it all we can.

There are many things a person can do to mess up a relationship, and for each of those there is another choice that can be made that will strengthen one. You can cheat or you can remain faithful. You can lie or you can tell the truth. You can keep things inside yourself or you can communicate so that your partner knows how you feel. A person will work so much that they build an impressive career, and another will forego the extra work so they can build a stronger family. One person will spend all their free time with their friends and the next person spends it all with their family, while a third balances the two and is probably the better off for it. For each decision we make that strengthens the relationship we have, we become better people, and we live better lives. Chrystel and I have made a commitment to live better lives by treating each other better. We talk, we give and take some, and we reach an agreement most of the time. We compromise where we need to, communicate as we should and we stand together in a stronger relationship because of it.

Final thoughts

I recently read a book written by Colin Fletcher detailing his hike of the length of the Grand Canyon National Park back in 1963. The book, titled The Man Who Walked Through Time[i], begins with Colin, at forty years old, seeing the Grand Canyon for the first time in his life and being mesmerized by it's beauty and grandeur. A year later, he hiked the Canyon from one end of the National Park to the other, and along the two-month journey he discovered as much about himself and man's place in the world as he did about the Canyon. Toward the end of his journey, he pondered that "there is a powerful human compulsion to leave things tied up in neat little bundles. But every journey except your last has an open end. And any journey of value is above all a chapter in a personal odyssey."

Life is a journey in its own right. As I look back on the chapters that make up this book, I see them as chapters in my life. I see the mistakes that I made and the lessons I learned from them. I understand the problems that we all grapple with, to succeed, to survive, to find love and friendship, to make our mark on the world. I see where the decisions I made shaped who I am today, but did not solely define me. I am much more than the mistakes I made. I am more than the lessons I learned in the school of hard knocks.

I know what it is like to make a ton of mistakes in my life, from ones that cost me money to those that cost me friendships. You can take my advice or not, but I have told you these things because I have traveled down these roads and they are not easy ones to follow. I know what it is like to make these mistakes because I lived them. But like Colin Fletcher, I know that life is a journey and I am not at the end of it. The chapters are still being written. I am human, so I will make more mistakes. But I will learn from them, as I learned from the ones in my past and I will try to not repeat the same ones over again. I have shared my experiences with you so perhaps you will not make the same mistakes I did. I want you to make simpler ones that don't cost you as much as mine cost me, but in the end, the choice is yours. You will make mistakes, and you will have to take responsibility for them. Your life is your journey, and your mistakes are your own.

---

[i] Fletcher, Colin. The Man Who Walked Through Time. New York: Random House, 1968

Printed in the United States
by Baker & Taylor Publisher Services